Long Trek To India And Freedom

Long Trek To India And Freedom

(Daring escape by three Indian Army Officers from Japanese POW Camp)

by

Brig Jasbir Singh, SM

Vij Books India Pvt Ltd
New Delhi (India)

Published by

Vij Books India Pvt Ltd

(Publishers, Distributors & Importers)
2/19, Ansari Road, Darya Ganj
New Delhi - 110002
Phones: 91-11-43596460, 91-11- 47340674
Fax: 91-11-47340674
e-mail : vijbooks@rediffmail.com
web: www.vijbooks.com

Copyright © 2014, Brig Jasbir Singh

First Published in India: 2014

Paperback Edition 2015

No part of this book may be reproduced, stored in a retrieval system, transmitted or utilised in any form or by any means, electronic, mechanical, photocopying, recording or otherwise, without the prior permission of the copyright owner. Application for such permission should be addressed to the publisher.

CONTENTS

Author's Note		ix
Prologue		xiv
Chapter 1	— Operations in Malaya & Singapore (December 1940 - February 1942)	1
Chapter 2	— Captivity and Escape	31
Chapter 3	— 'Green Hell' (Thailand to Burma)	60
Chapter 4	— Ordeal at Monywa (Burma)	82
Chapter 5	— Onwards to India	92
Conclusion		110

Appendices

Appendix 'A'	— Evasion By Capt GS Parab After Battle of Slim River	115
Appendix 'B'	— Addresses made at Singapore (17 February 1942).	117
Appendix 'C'	— Letter from Gen AE Wavell, Commander-in-Chief in India, to Capt Balbir Singh, MC.	120
Appendix 'D'	— Brief History of Azad Hind Fauj / Indian National Army (INA)	121

Maps

Map-1	:	Action at Chemor – 26 December 1941	11
Map-2	:	Battle of Slim River	18
Map-3	:	Japanese Attacks on Singapore Island	22
Map-4	:	Japanese Landings – Singapore	23
Map-5	:	Escape Route : Singapore to India [Singapore to Prachu-ab-Khirikan Section]	57
Map-6	:	Thailand to Burma	65
Map-7	:	Escape Route : Singapore to India [Monywa to Sumprabaum Section]	113
Map-8	:	Route Travelled by Air : Burma to India	108

Illustrations

Ill-1	:	Watercolour – Captured at Monywa (Book Cover)	
Ill-2	:	Watercolour – NCO of 4/19 Hyderabad Regt at Singapore (Sept 1939) (Book Rear Cover)	
Ill-2	:	Photo-Capt (later Brig) Balbir Singh	x
Ill-3	:	Photo-Capt (later Col) GS Parab	x
Ill-4	:	Photo-Capt(later Brig) Pritam Singh	x
Ill-5	:	Photo-Officers and VCOs of 4/19 Hyderabad Regt on eve of Departure for Singapore – 1939	xvii
Ill-6	:	Photo-An Allied patrol moves through Malayan jungle - 1940	xxi
Ill-7	:	Photo – Beach at Kota Bharu – Japanese Landing	3

Contents

		site (Dec 1941)	
Ill-8	:	Photo – Capt MG Jilani, Adjutant	7
Ill-9	:	Photo – Capt Balbir Singh, OC 'B' Coy	7
Ill-10	:	Watercolour – Attack on Bridge-head at Machang	8
Ill-6	:	Watercolour – Japanese attack at Chemor	12
Ill-7	:	Watercolour – Escape from Singapore	56
lll-8	:	Watercolour - To India at last	105
Ill-9	:	Photo – Military Cross	113
Ill-10	:	Photo – Veterans of Operations of 4/19 Hyderabad Regt (now 4 Kumaon) in Malaya & Singapore, at Ranikhet (INDIA) - 8 April 1961	114

AUTHOR'S NOTE

This is the little known story of a daring escape, by three young officers of Indian Army (IA), from a Japanese World War II Prisoner of War (POW) Camp, and their torturous trek to India and freedom. The trio escaped from POW Camp in Singapore in May 1942 and made their way through Malaya (now Malaysia), Thailand and Burma (now Myanmar), to reach India. In Burma they split into two groups. Balbir & Parab moved north through Myitkyina and enemy-held territories, before they contacted an allied patrol in the heavily jungled, hill tracts of upper Burma. They were flown from Sumprabum (Burma) to Tinsukia (India). Capt Pritam Singh, meanwhile proceeded west from Monywa. He crossed the front-lines and entered India at Manipur. Capt (later Brig) Balbir Singh and Capt (later Col) GS Parab belonged to 4/19 Hyderabad Regiment (now Fourth Battalion, The Kumaon Regiment or 4 Kumaon) while the third officer, Capt (later Brig) Pritam Singh (originally from 4/19 Hyderabad Regiment), was from 5/16 Punjab Regiment and later Parachute Regt[1]. The book is a tribute to my father, Brig Balbir Singh, MC, who had master-minded the exciting escape from POW Camp at Singapore and the incredible six months long journey to India.

All three officers served with honour in Indian Army (IA) and led remarkable lives[2]. Sadly, none of the three is alive today, but their daring

---

1 Later, during fighting in Kashmir (*1947 - 48 Operations*) Pritam commanded 1 KUMAON (PARA) [now 3 PARA]. He led the Unit past Hajipir Pass and into Poonch. Here, he remained surrounded by enemy forces for more than one year, beat back many enemy attacks and was promoted to rank of Brig. He is rightly known as '*Savior of Poonch*', and today, his yellowing photograph proudly adorns many homes in the border town.

2 Parab's son Anil G Parab, was commissioned in 4 Kumaon in 1967. An outstanding officer Maj AG Parab met an untimely end in an unfortunate firing accident (3.5 inch Rocket Launcher) on 21 January 1973, near Dimapur, Nagaland. . It was a sad loss for the

Capt (later Brig) Balbir Singh, MC

Capt (later Col) GS Parab, MC

Capt (later Brig) Pritam Singh, MC

AUTHOR'S NOTE

escapade has touched many lives and is often quoted as a saga of sheer guts, grit and determination. The long journey through enemy controlled areas, was undertaken on foot, elephants, rail, bus, boat and finally by air. While undertaking their long and difficult journey to India, the trio had great adventures and also suffered incredible privations and hardships. All their difficulties were endured with exemplary courage and fortitude. During their long trek to India, the officers were re-captured by the Japanese enemy, on two occasions.

Despite intense torture after their first arrest at Monywa (Burma), they succeeded in convincing their captors they were helpless civilians, with the help of their well rehearsed story. During their passage through Burma, they pretended to be innocent refugees who had been displaced from their homes by the awful war! Luckily, in Monywa the Japanese Military Police (Kemptai) reluctantly believed their incredible story and after a torturous fortnight in custody, they were put on a train going back to Pegu. After undergoing terrible Japanese brutality in Monywa, on their release the escapees split into two groups. Balbir and Parab proceeded north to Myitkina. They had planned to contact Allied forces in upper Burma. On the other hand, Pritam wanted to take the shorter route. He was prepared to hazard a passage through the front-lines in western Burma and Manipur (India). They had realized that three escapees moving together were very 'visible' and thus vulnerable to capture. On the second occasion, Balbir and Parab were captured by an enemy patrol near the front-lines in Upper Burma, near Myitkyina. They spent only a night in custody, and while they were being taken to a regular enemy camp, both the officers crashed into the dense jungle, and escaped. The enemy fired some desultory rifle shots, which resulted in further speeding the escapees' onwards in their flight.

In 1988, nearly half a century after their escape, Balbir retraced his footsteps along the route they had traversed in 1942. Many of the brave-hearts who had generously assisted them with money, shelter and vital information, had passed away. Balbir returned money the escapees had borrowed during the escapade and profusely thanked the surviving

---

officer's family, 4 Kumaon and IA. Balbir's son, Jasbir Singh, was also commissioned in 4 Kumaon in December 1970.

relatives. Especially touching was Balbir's meeting with the daughter of Khan Zaman, the Pathan cattle smuggler, who had lived with his Thai wife at Prachu-ab-Khirikan, on east coast of Thailand. The Pathan had liberally helped them on their way from Thailand to Burma. Khan Zaman and his wife had both passed away, but their daughter, who had been a bubbly, little girl in May 1942, spent time chatting with Balbir. She told him, a Japanese patrol had come to Prachu-ab-Khirikan with Thai policemen, a few days after they had left the town. The Japanese had gathered all inhabitants of Prachu together and announced the three Allied escapees had been recaptured and shot dead. They seemed to know of the assistance provided to the escapees and warned the people of dire consequences, if they helped any escaped prisoners. The lady had added, the Japanese announcement had greatly saddened both her parents, who would often talk about the three escapees in glowing terms.

Brig Balbir Singh, MC, passed away at Command Hospital, Chandimandir in January 2004. I could learn few details about the escape during my father's lifetime, as he rarely spoke about their great adventure. However, I was told he had delivered an interesting talk in Staff College, Quetta, (now in Pakistan) in 1944, and later he wrote a couple of fascinating articles in Journal of The Kumaon Regiment. Thus, I managed to piece together the incredible story, after listening to my father's rare descriptions of the 'escape' and on reading the articles he had written. Col GS Parab also wrote a short account of their 'escape'. When I had talked about Parab's account with my father, he recounted a few more interesting details of their travels. In 1976, a few years after I had been commissioned in 4 Kumaon, I undertook a trip to Singapore, Malaysia, Thailand and Burma. During this trip I generally followed the route that was taken by the escapees. I was thus, able to get a close feel of their incredible adventures. I sincerely thank Col (retired) Narendra Singh, Commanding Officer (CO) of 4 Kumaon (1978 to 1981), for obtaining a copy of Balbir's Interrogation Report [CSDIC (India), Red Fort, Delhi, (No 2 Section Report No 16, dated 2 November, 1942)] from London (UK), in 2007. The Report contains a wealth of information about the escape and trek to India. I have used the 'Interrogation Report' quite liberally, while writing this book.

AUTHOR'S NOTE

The book titled '*Long Trek to India and Freedom*' has been put together after receiving valuable inputs from Lt Gen (retired) MS Shergill, PVSM, AVSM, Vr C, ADC, about various personalities who have been mentioned in the book, and some others, as well. I thank Christopher Bayly and Tim Harper for inputs from their extensively researched book named '*Forgotten Armies*'. Their book has provided me with much, valuable information about operations in Malaya & Singapore, and life in the prisoner of war (POW) camps.

With great pride, I dedicate the book '*Long Trek to India and Freedom*', to my father, Brig Balbir Singh, MC, of 4/19 Hyderabad Regt (now 4 Kumaon).

September 2013   Brig Jasbir Singh

'*Valley View Villa*'   brig.jasbir.singh@gmail.Com
Village Naini, P.O. Kalika,
Ranikhet - 263645,
District Almora (UK),
INDIA.

[Telephones – 9760000014 & 05966-240266]

PROLOGUE

Historical Background

4/19 Hyderabad Regiment, (now called 4 Kumaon) has had a long and interesting history, since it was raised by Nawab Salabat Khan in 1788. After it was raised in Ellichpore (now Achalpur, Maharashtra), the Unit has had a enviable record of operational service in India, China (1900-1901), East Africa (1914-1915), Afghanistan (1919), Iraq (1923-1924) and Gaza, UAR (1959-1960). A major earthquake struck Quetta on the night of 31 May 1935. The earthquake caused untold damage and destruction in Quetta. For its stellar role during relief operations, the Unit received a *Citation of Merit* from Lord Willingdon, Viceroy of India. In addition, L Nk Mata Din was awarded the Empire Gallantry Medal (later converted to recently instituted 'George Cross'. The medal was awarded for great gallantry shown by Mata Din while he rescued two civilians who were buried deep in the rubble.

From Quetta, the unit moved to Secunderabad. Here, the Unit was part of the local garrison, and had a company deployed at Bolarum. On 4 December 1937, the unit was presented with Colours by Lt Gen JES Brind, KCB, KBE, CMG, DSO, GOC-in-C Southern Command, during a glittering military parade. The Colours were received by Indian officers for the first time[1]. With the worsening world political situation, in August 1939, the unit moved by rail to Madras (now Chennai) and sailed as part of 12 Indian Infantry Brigade [*Force 'EMU'*]. Other Infantry battalions of the brigade were 2nd Battalion, Argyll & Sutherland Highlanders (A & SH)

---

1 The two Indian officers who received the Colours were Capt K Bhagwati Singh and Capt Dilsukh Maan. Today, 4/19 Hyderabad Regiment is known as 4th Battalion, The Kumaon Regiment (or 4 Kumaon). The Unit is flag bearer amongst highly decorated Infantry battalions of Indian Army, with India's first PVC and three post-Independence Battle Honours. On 8 April 1961, 4 Kumaon became the first Unit to receive President's Colours in India, after Independence. The Colours were presented Dr Rajendra Prasad (India's first President) to Capt (later Maj Gen) DPS Raghuvanshi, at Ranikhet (Uttarakhand).

and 5/2nd Punjab Regt. In those days, sealed orders bearing destination of the unit/formation were opened by the Commanding Officer (CO), only after their ship had left harbour and was on the high seas! In this particular case, the formation's destination was the island of Singapore.

Capt SM Shrinagesh (later Gen and Chief of Army Staff) was Adjutant, and Capt M Azam Khan (later Lt Gen & Governor of East Pakistan) was Quarter Master (QM) of the Unit. Shrinagesh was posted to India in December 1939 and he handed over duties of Adjutant to Capt (later Maj Gen & Adjutant General of Pakistan Army) MG Jilani. Maj KS Thimayya (later Gen and Chief of Army Staff) was commanding 'D' Company. On its arrival in Singapore, the Unit was accommodated in tents pitched on the grounds of Tanglin, till the construction of wooden hutments had been completed at Tyersall Park.

Besides 4/19 Hyderabad Regiment, Tyersall Park also housed HQ 12 Indian Infantry Brigade, A & SH and 12 Indian General Hospital. After outbreak of World War II, units were being rapidly raised in India for their subsequent move to Middle East Sector (Egypt). Older units like 4/19 Hyderabad Regiment were asked to repatriate some experienced troops, who were to form the nucleus of newly raised battalions'.

Preparations for War

Malaya[2] (now Malaysia), was a British colony. It consisted of a number of independent states, which were ruled by Sultans. The population was a mix of numerous races. The majority of people were indigenous Malays, however, there were also Europeans, Indians (mainly Tamils & Sikhs) and Chinese. Singapore was a modern, cosmopolitan island city. It compared favourably with most larger sized cities of the world. Singapore was a very pleasant place, when the Battalion arrived from India[3]. There were good hotels and a lot of social activity. People of Indian descent were particularly happy to see an Indian Unit in Singapore. Some officers bought cars[4] and

---

2   At the time, the island city of Singapore formed part of Malaya.

3   Singapore was a 'duty free' port with a favourable currency exchange rate. One 'Singapore Dollar' equaled 1 ½ Indian Rupees (Rs). Delighted young officers compared the price of goods, with the basic cost of Scotch Whisky – in Secunderabad a bottle of Scotch Whisky had cost Rs 8 ¼ , while in Singapore it was for only Rs 5 – so, life was bliss!

4   Capt Balbir Singh bought a small car (Morris-8), and toured extensively across Malaya.

OFFICERS & VCOs OF 4/19 HYDERABAD REGT AT SECUNDERABAD (1939) [EVE OF DEPARTURE FOR SINGAPORE]

PROLOGUE

SITTING (L to R) : Maj MI Majid, Maj (later Gen & COAS) SM Shrinagesh, VCO, Not Known (NK), Lt Col Douglas Stewart (CO), Sub Maj, Ujjala Singh, NK, VCO, Maj (later Col in INA & India's Ambassador) Niranjan Singh Gill.

STANDING (1st Row, L to R) : Maj (later Lt Gen in Pak Army & Governor of East Pakistan) M Azam Khan, Capt (MC and killed in Battle of Singapore) LJC Lind, Maj (later DSO, Padma Vibhushan, General, COAS & UN Commander in Cyprus) KS Thimayya, Maj (later OBE, Lt Gen & Governor) K Bahadur Singh, Capt (later MC & Brig) Balbir Singh, Capt (Gold Medal & Five Sports Blues from Royal Military College, Sandhurst & later Brig) Apji Randhir Singh, Lt Balwant Singh (later bayoneted to death in a POW Camp in Borneo), Capt (later MC, Brig & *Saviour of Poonch*) Pritam Singh, Capt (IC-1 & later Maj Gen) K Bhagwati Singh, Lt (killed during Battle of Slim River, Malaya) KD Vasudeva, Lt (killed during Battle of Slim River, Malaya) GK Mehta, NK.

STANDING (Top Row, L to R) : VCO, NK, NK, Lt Dilsukh Maan, 2 Lt (later, MVC and Lt Gen) MM Khanna, Lt (later Maj Gen in Pak Army) MG Jilani, VCO, VCO, Lt Judge, Lt (killed at Chemor, Malaya) VW Harris, VCO.   :

toured Malaya, while others even visited the historic temples at Ankor Wat, in Cambodia (now Kampuchea). It was a popular affair for officers to visit *Sea View Hotel* on Sunday mornings, for a game of badminton or tennis. Later, they would have a leisurely breakfast on the wide terrace, while watching huge breakers come crashing onto the shore. It was at *Sea View Hotel,* where after the fall of France, the atmosphere would often be surcharged with emotion. British men and women would stand up and sing in chorus, the well known wartime song, *'There will always be England; and England shall be free…'*. Tears would often flow from the eyes of many a young woman in the gathering!

The grounds of nearby Raffles College were used for training activities, as well as sports. For jungle training, the Unit did not always need to go to mainland of Malaya, as in those days Singapore itself had thick jungles that provided good training facilities. Thailand had a poorly demarcated border with Malaya. The border runs along thick jungles and low hills. The Malayan peninsula has a spine of hilly terrain with thick jungles on either side. There are relatively flat coastal plains, intersected by numerous rivers. Malaya has tropical climate with heavy rainfall all round the year. Swampy areas near rivers and the relatively flat coastal plains are intersected by numerous sluggish rivers. The swampy areas are choked with dense undergrowth and many rivers have muddy water that flows to the open sea.

Vines and creepers generally hung from the trees and made visibility and movement difficult in the jungle. Large areas were under rubber plantations, and the large rubber trees added to the problems of poor visibility. Movement across country was problematic, and it was only possible along the fields of paddy or through pine-apple cultivations. Overall, the terrain was difficult for operations and posed immense logistics problems. Due to the availability of natural cover, the tropical jungle was ideally suited for infiltration, ambush and sneak attacks.

His knowledge of the countryside came in handy during later operations and his escape to India. After the unit had moved north for operations, the car was lost in wartime chaos. However, much later, in 1950, Balbir (then Sub-Area Commander, Jalandhar) was pleasantly surprised to receive a letter from Singapore Police informing him that his car had been found and sold. The letter also contained a cheque of sale proceeds of the Morris car!

Prologue

Singapore Island lies at the southern tip of Malayan peninsula and it was linked to the mainland, with a strong causeway. The Island was the bastion of British power in the Far East and it had been converted into a virtual fortress by spending over 60 million pounds on its defences. There were sufficient stocks of ammunition, rations and water to sustain operations for at least six months. The Island was strongly guarded and had coastal batteries for defence against hostile naval landings. It had been appreciated that Singapore would be attacked from the sea-ward side, an eventuality for which the island fortress was well prepared. In the less likely eventuality of a land-based offensive, it had been appreciated that Japanese landings could take place at Singora and Patani beaches in neutral Thailand. Thus, detailed reconnaissance had been conducted and a plan ('*Operation 'Matador'*) had been prepared, to immediately send troops into Thailand to cover both the beaches. Ironically, the landings took place at these very beaches, but the plans to send troops to contest the Japanese, were inexplicably never implemented. Japanese landings were initially resisted by Thai Army units, while Allied formations in north Malaya waited at the Malaya -Thailand border to see what would happen! It was a case of complete inaction, while the Japanese were able to land, totally unchallenged![5]

In a major departure from the general thinking at the time, Lt Col D Stuart, CO, 4/19 Hyderabad Regiment, was certain the Japanese would land at the beaches and then surge through the thick Malayan jungles towards Singapore. Though Stuart was ridiculed and looked at with contempt, he ensured the unit trained hard for jungle warfare, at various locations on the Malayan peninsula. There was much to learn and officers ensured that troops gained confidence to operate independently among the trees and heavy undergrowth. Troops learnt to move silently through primary jungles, however, in secondary jungle often a path had to be cut to allow movement of troops. However, all movement made a lot of noise and progress of troops was extremely slow. Sometimes, it took a whole day to advance a mere 10 km! During jungle training, troops were horrified to find themselves covered with brown or black, shiny leeches. They soon

---

[5] The British commanders did not initially activate Operation Matador as it was felt the Japanese would be provoked to launch large scale operations. When they wanted to launch the operation, Japanese landings had already taken place!

learned to remove the leeches by touching them with the lighted end of a bidi[6].

Survival in the jungle was an important aspect of the training that was conducted. Obtaining drinking water was one of the biggest problems for survival in the jungle. Troops were taught how to find fresh water by cutting 'lianas' that festooned the trees in the jungle. The water which dripped from the severed end of 'lianas', was clear, cold and did not have an unpleasant taste. The jungle was teeming with wild animals of various kinds. They were quite friendly unless attacked, and they generally kept out of the way of troops. Monkeys normally followed the soldiers and chattered shrilly high in the trees. The troops were happy to have the monkeys near them, as they would give a shrill warning of any approaching animal predators or humans. Such a warning was invaluable, as it disclosed the move of enemy patrols in the thick jungles. Many types of snakes were encountered in the jungle. However hard the officers and men tried, they could not overcome their loathing towards the slimy reptiles.

An Allied patrol moves through the Malayan jungle - 1940

---

6 'Bidi' is a local, Indian cigarette that provides smoked intoxication to the user. 'Bidis' are commonly used by troops of the sub-continent. In a 'bidi', tobacco is tightly wrapped in a leaf, lit at the end and smoked like a cigarette.

CHAPTER 1

OPERATIONS IN MALAYA AND SINGAPORE
(DECEMBER 1941 - FEBRUARY 1942)

'While I do not underestimate the fighting qualities of Japanese soldiers, I know our men have been more than a match for them, whenever we have met on equal terms'.

Capt Balbir Singh, MC
(Answering a question on fighting qualities of Japanese soldiers, after a talk on 'Escape from Singapore', at Staff College, Quetta – 1944)

Code-word *'Gloves-off'*

4/19 Hyderabad Regt had moved from Singapore on 1 December 1941 to Mantien, for jungle warfare training. During the early hours of 7 December, long lines of tired troops returned to their tented camp near Mantien after a grueling exercise along the coast. They had hacked their way through thick coastal jungles for three nights and everyone was quite exhausted. The men had barely settled down to get some sleep, when at around 2 AM a message was received by the wireless-set operator on duty. The simple message contained code-words of *'Gloves Off'*. When the tired troops were shaken awake, they thought orders had been received for conducting yet more jungle training! Gravity of the situation did not immediately register on the weary minds d with of troops, till everyone was assembled and told that hostilities had commenced with Japan! At once, there was great excitement in the air and HQs began to buzz with activity. The unit was not permitted to return to Singapore, to pick up any additional gear. They would go into battle with whatever they had carried for the exercise and return to their unit lines at Tyersall Park as prisoners of war (POW), after heavy fighting down the Malayan peninsula and on Singapore Island.

However, the officers and men were glad that the operations would finally be beginning, putting an end to the wretched jungle training moves and the endless wait for operations to commence! At Battalion HQ, the ponderous wireless sets were switched '*on*' and communications were established with HQ 12 Indian Infantry Brigade and other units of the formation [5/2 Punjab Regt and 2 Argyll & Sutherland Highlanders (A & SH)].

Early next morning (8 December 1941), the Unit entrained in two special trains and proceeded up the Malayan peninsula, to Kuala Krai. This was the first of many moves the Unit would undertake in action filled days that lay ahead. The situation was indeed grim, and heavy fighting was expected. Troops had heard startling reports of Japanese brutalities in China. There were immediate reports of Japanese landings[1] in Kota Bahru area and events were unfolding at an alarming pace. Japanese landings in Thailand and north Malaya had jolted the Allies into taking immediate action. Thus, 12 Infantry Brigade was ordered to hold the advancing Japanese forces from hastily prepared defensive positions, near Kota Bahru. The Allies had realized the enemy advance had to be halted without delay, so that forward troops could be withdrawn and re-grouped. Thus, the Unit arrived at Kuala Krai during early hours of 9 December. Dismounting from the trains, the troops loaded in vehicles and immediately moved to Ketereh, which was 12 miles south of Kota Bahru. During their advance along narrow jungle tracks, some Japanese troops moved on bicycles laden with immediately needed supplies and ammunition. This innovative method of advance allowed for rapid movement, as the troops were not slowed by sluggish logistics elements. The Allies tried to slow the enemy's advance by demolishing bridges and larger culverts, but the wily Japanese quickly threw up improvised foot bridges and shocked the Allies by continuing with their rapid advance.

---

1 A Planter named Bill Bangs, on a French-owned Rubber Plantation, had enlisted in the 'Frontier Patrol' and in early December 1941 he proceeded to Yala in Southern Thailand, in disguise. From here he moved to Patani. His 'boy' overheard drunken Japanese in a bar in Naratiwat boasting about an invasion that would happen on the next day. Alarmed, Bill Bangs had raced to the border, but he was detained there by Thai border guards. He escaped across the river in a sampan and passed the vital information to the British commander in Kota Bahru. But, it was too late, for as he retired to bed in an exhausted state Bangs heard initial gunshots of the first land battle of the great Asian war. Though, the invasion of Malaya had commenced, the surprise attack on Pearl Harbour was still several hours away!

There was heavy fighting around Kota Bahru, an elements of 8 Infantry Brigade kept falling back under severe enemy pressure. By 7.30 PM on 9 December, the battalion had occupied defences with good fields of fire that could properly cover the surrounding scrub land and paddy fields. A Battery of 4.5 inch Howitzers (three guns) had been placed in direct support of the Unit.

Japanese 'Battle Flag'

Beach at Kota Bahru – one of the Japanese landing sites (December 1941)

First Contact with Japanese – 10 December 1941

During the night of 9 December, forward troops kept falling back in utter disarray. Though, commanders tried to keep a firm grip on troops, tensions and uncertainty continued to mount. Fortunately, no enemy troops appeared during the night. On the next morning, the defences were re-adjusted. But, there was little rest for troops who remained nervous and expected the Japanese forward elements to show up at any time. The weather, however, was cool and humid as intermittent showers had continued through the night.

The night of 10 December was totally dark and it kept drizzling steadily. The light rain had dampened the helmets and grim faces of soldiers in their trenches. Troops peered into the darkness and clutched their weapons tightly. Far away from India and their homes, they stood in their trenches and nervously awaited the Japanese attack. There was a constant hum of crickets and other jungle insects. First contact was made with advancing elements of 'Takumi Force' at about 9 PM. The situation quickly became confused, as about 60 Japanese soldiers armed with light

Kota Bharu, (Malaya),1941. A decoy Lockheed Hudson aircraft at RAF Base, Kota Bharu. Such decoys deceived the Japanese and invited their air attacks, at inaccurate locations.

machine guns (LMGs) and rifles, emerged from the jungle and attacked the unit's forward companies, with support of medium mortars. The enemy was lightly clad and equipped. Exploding mortar bombs made a lot of noise, but the Japanese fire was erratic and did not cause much damage.

Only a few men sustained light shrapnel wounds. A number of times during the night, forward companies asked for artillery support and 80 rounds were fired by the Howitzer Battery. Heavy firing of small arms by forward troops continued till early hours of the morning. Troops remained jittery in the darkness and each company reported it was either being outflanked or attacked. As quickly as they had appeared, the enemy faded away and further attacks ceased. As daylight increased, the defensive positions were re-adjusted. The first encounter with Japanese was an encouraging one. The Unit had managed to hold their positions and suffered only a few casualties. After meeting with stiff opposition from the defenders, the enemy had broken contact, and hastily withdrawn to regroup, before launching renewed assaults.

Rearguard Action at Machang

On 11 December, 8 Infantry Brigade had been ordered to withdraw to Machang and move across a steel girder bridge that spanned the Kelantan River. 4/19 Hyderabad Regt had been ordered to fight a rearguard action and allow 8 Brigade to break contact with the enemy. The move was carried out smoothly, except for a daring enemy 'jitter party', that infiltrated 3/17th Dogras and opened fire. Despite enemy's firing, the Brigade continued to withdraw. After a while, the enemy party fell silent and it was assumed they had moved away. The Brigade had almost completely crossed the bridge and moved south of Machang. Only a company of 1/10th Baluch Regt and 'B' Company of 4/19 Hyderabad Regt were yet to cross the bridge, when an enemy 'jitter party' opened fire on the Baluchis. The bridge had been prepared for demolition and on hearing firing at close range an alarmed Sapper depressed the handle of the exploder-dynamo set, and blew up the bridge. There were a series of deafening explosions and large portions of the iron-girder bridge slid into the water, leaving the two companies stranded on the enemy side of Kelantan River. In absence of any other option, the companies stranded across the river wisely took up hasty defensive positions, and formed a shallow bridge-head. The thick jungle and poor visibility around the bridge-head made the position extremely vulnerable to probes by the enemy.

In the dark of night, CO of 4/19 Hyderabad Regt with a couple of officers (including Capt MG Jilani, Adjutant), went across Kelantan River by boat to inspect the bridge-head positions and instill confidence in troops across the river. Enemy engaged the boat with small arms fire and heavy mortars. Mortar bombs exploded in the river sending tall geysers of water into the air, but the boat safely made the river crossing. Capt Balbir Singh, Company Commander of 'B' Company and two soldiers were waiting at the far bank to receive the boat. A few Japanese mortar bombs exploded nearby, while Balbir was briefing CO about the bridge-head defences. The CO's party, accompanied by Balbir, went around the perimeter defences of both the companies. On seeing the CO and officers among them, the men raised their fists and cheered lustily. Morale sky-rocketed and troops stood ready to face the enemy's attacks. The neighbouring *Baluchis* were also upbeat on seeing the *Hyderabad's* CO and his party in their midst.

It was an action filled night and many intense fire-fights broke out along the perimeter, as the enemy made repeated attempts to assault the bridge-head.

However, each time the enemy tried to dislodge the bridge-head, the attacks were beaten back with casualties. As the frequency of enemy attacks was increasing, Balbir left CO's party and returned to his improvised command post to direct the desperate battle. Troops fought bravely and did not permit the Japanese to break into the bridge-head. The fight went on all night, with remainder of the brigade providing fire-support from across the river. During the early hours of morning, intense firing suddenly broke out from three sides of the bridge-head, leading to a difficult tactical situation. The enemy fired a number of star-shells to illuminate the defences, before launching further attacks. To make matters worse, wireless communications between 'B' Company and Battalion HQ had broken down. As the fire of one enemy mortar was very accurate, 'B' Company suffered 13 casualties (seven killed and six wounded), from mortar bombs exploding among the shallow trenches. However, all Japanese attempts to gain a foot-hold on the perimeter, were effectively foiled.

Capt MG Jilani, Adjutant. *Capt Balbir Singh, OC 'B' Company.*

As dawn was breaking on 12 December, troops who were stranded across Kelantan River, received orders to move to the home bank. It was a difficult pre-dawn operation, as the troops were moved across the river in country boats, under the cover of heavy mortar concentrations. Wounded men were placed at bottom of the boats while being taken across the river. All the boats successfully made a number of hazardous crossings and the operation was successfully completed. Each time the boats were rowed across the river, the enemy brought down heavy fire on them. However, the enemy's fire did not hit any of the boats and there were no losses during the crossings.

*'B'Company beats back Japanese attacks on the bridgehead at Machang –
11 December 1941*

Further Withdrawals

Next morning, (13 December), urgent local administration tasks, like washing of clothes and cooking a hot meal were being carried out, when a massive Japanese air raid struck Krai. This was the Unit's first experience of an air raid. Men dived for cover as bombs screamed into Krai and exploded with shattering bangs. One bomb exploded in the Battalion area and a number of fuel drums were hurled high into the sky, before going up in flames. Luckily, only one Sep received injuries from bomb shrapnel. After the Japanese aircraft had departed, the badly shaken troops repeatedly looked up at the sky, as they hurriedly completed the administrative chores. Next morning, orders were received to occupy the south bank of Nal River at Sungei Nal. The Unit held a six mile long frontage for the next two nights, and prevented the enemy from making either a crossing or any move along Nal River in boats.

Japanese Infantry on the move

During this period, Japanese reconnaissance aircraft constantly flew overhead and there was a marked increase in enemy patrolling activity. On 17 December, 4/19 Hyderabad Regt was relieved at Nal River position, and it marched back to Krai. The Battalion entrained at 8 PM and finally steamed out of Kelantan Area. On the morning of 23 December, heavy enemy air raids struck Perak Area and a number of the Unit's trucks were destroyed in the air attacks. The neighbouring unit, (A & SH) suffered heavily and sustained 20 casualties. While the air raid was taking place, Japanese infantry rapidly infiltrated through the thick jungle. The enemy build-up along Kroh - Kuala Kangsar Road was so quick that 11 Infantry Division, which was located ahead, was forced to fall back. Consequently, 12 Infantry Brigade was ordered to withdraw at midnight to avoid being surrounded by the enemy.

Action at Chemor (See Map 1)

A defensive position was taken up at Chemor, on 24 December 1941. 5/2nd Punjab Regt was deployed ahead, while 4/19 Hyderabad Regt and A & SH were held in depth. An ambitious plan had been formulated to lure the enemy into a trap and cause its annihilation. On being attacked, 5/2nd Punjab Regt was to withdraw to a designated line. Then, the enemy was to be destroyed with the use of timed artillery barrages. To lure the enemy into the trap, 'D' Company of 4/19 Hyderabad Regt was to deploy on a feature called 'Limestone Rock'. Once the trap had been sprung the Unit was to prevent the enemy from escaping by engaging with MG and 3-inch mortar fire. Zero-Hour was fixed at 9.15 AM on 26 December.

After the demoralizing withdrawals, finally a victory was expected at Chemor and everyone was upbeat. At 7.30 AM, 'D' Company started out for 'Limestone Rock'. As anticipated, the Japanese attack on 5/2nd Punjab, commenced on time. But, soon the situation got out of hand. By approximately 8.45 AM, the enemy had pushed 5/2nd Punjab well beyond the designated limit of withdrawal, and was following closely behind the withdrawing Punjabis. The planned artillery barrages were not fired as the enemy had moved beyond the designated 'killing ground' and remained in contact with 5/2nd Punjab. Heavy firing was also heard from 'Limestone Rock'. It was apparent the ambitious plan had misfired. Since, the vital artillery bombardments could not be fired, the operation was called off by Brigade HQ. CO realized that 'D' Company had to be urgently retrieved, before they clashed with the enemy and suffered serious casualties. However, there was no way to inform 'D' Company as it did not have wireless communications with Battalion HQ. Thus, two bicycle-mounted Despatch Riders (DRs) were sent to convey the urgent message to 'D' Company, followed by a section of troops and lastly three armoured carriers. All three attempts to contact 'D' Company proved unsuccessful. It was later known that the enemy had surrounded 'D' Company and some very heavy fighting had taken place. Severe casualties had been inflicted on the enemy, before 'D' Company was overrun and finally decimated. Most men were killed, while a few men were captured. There were no survivors and 'D' Company, 4/19 Hyderabad Regt ceased to exist on 26 December 1941.

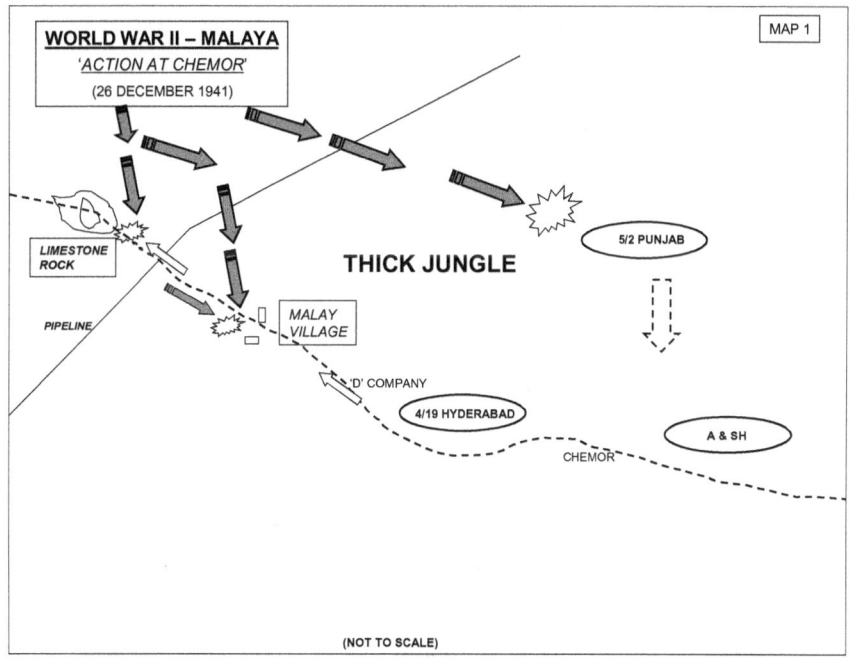

After the disaster at Chemor, orders were passed for 4/19 Hyderabad Regt and A & SH to withdraw to Gopeng. 5/2nd Punjab had already been withdrawn. However, the enemy had other plans! At 4.45 PM, Japanese moved around eastern edge of 'Limestone Rock' and attacked 'B' Company, just as it commenced its withdrawal. The troops had rapidly re-occupied their positions and engaged the assaulting enemy. 'B' Company beat back two Japanese attacks and inflicted serious casualties on the enemy. The mauled enemy pulled back and did not attempt to interfere any further with the company's withdrawal. Two men of 'B' Company were seriously wounded and were carried back on improvised stretchers. One of the wounded jawans succumbed to his wounds at Advanced Dressing Station (ADS). Thus, ended 26 December 1941 - a sad day in history of 4/19 Hyderabad Regt. Although no-one knew it then, a worse fate awaited the Battalion during the next action – Battle of Slim River.

Japanese Troops Attack 'D' Company 4/19 Hyderabad Regiment (Now 4 Kumaon) at Chemor (Malaya) on 26 Dec 1941

Withdrawal to Slim River

During that night, the Battalion (having only three rifle companies) was deployed at Gopeng, while A & SH took up a defensive position in depth. 'C' Company's position was located towards the enemy and 'A' Company dominated a bend in the road, about 800 yards to the rear. Battalion HQ was in Gopeng village while 'B' Company held the southern outskirts. At 1 PM on 27 December, Battalion HQ was heavily shelled. During afternoon, the enemy outflanked the Battalion and attacked A & SH. Sensing the enemy's encircling move, the Unit was quickly moved behind A & SH, leaving 'B' Company to hold the outskirts of Gopeng and cover the road. The Battalion moved to its new position under 2 IC, while CO stayed back with 'B' Company.

At about 10 PM, the enemy advanced from Gopeng and was engaged by 'B' Company under Capt Balbir Singh. Japanese infantry managed to reach within 30 or 40 yards from 'B' Company, before they were pushed back by heavy fire from the defenders. Loud tank noises were heard in the dark and enemy repeatedly sounded motor horns to intimidate the defenders. The action continued till orders were received at 2 AM, for 'B' Company to occupy a position behind A & SH. Moving in the dark through Japanese held areas, 'B' Company successfully disengaged from the enemy and rejoined the Unit.

On the next morning, volume of enemy artillery fire increased considerably and the Battalion sustained several casualties during the enemy shelling. Enemy tanks and infantry continued to out-flank the Unit from the south. At 11 AM, A & SH was withdrawn to a position further in depth. Within an hour of this re-deployment, forward elements of the enemy contacted the Battalion. Two Japanese cyclists, who were craftily leading the advance while dressed in Malay clothing, were shot dead. A heavily camouflaged car that was following the leading enemy cyclists was destroyed by ant-tank fire. The enemy halted and began to move around the northern flank, through thick, rubber plantations. At about 3.15 PM, the Japanese man-handled an anti-tank gun off the road and destroyed an Amoured Carrier (belonging to Unit), with a direct hit. Once again, orders were received to withdraw and stabilize the situation, as the enemy was outflanking the Unit in large numbers. It was perceived that enemy was trying to capture the nearby bridge at Dipang.

While the Japanese flanking movement was taking place, 4/19 Hyderabad withdrew over Dipang Bridge, followed by A & SH and 5/2nd Punjab Regt. Dipang Bridge was held by a Gurkha unit of 28 Infantry Brigade. 4/19 Hyderabad had by now been constantly in action with the rear-most brigade in Malaya, for about a month. The Unit had been fighting costly rearguard actions with 12 Indian Infantry Brigade, under strenuous and extremely difficult conditions. Thus, the Brigade was earmarked to move to Bidor for a few days of well-earned rest, and 28 Infantry Brigade was tasked to hold the enemy at Dipang. However, barely an hour after the Battalion had crossed Dipang Bridge the enemy attacked the Gurkha unit with infantry supported by tanks. 28 Infantry Brigade and 6/15 Brigade (amalgamated remnants of 6 and 15 Brigades) held the road leading south from Dipang, while 12 Infantry Brigade moved on to Bidor.

The next two days were spent digging defences to occupy a 'two-up' defensive position. The frontage allotted to the Unit was large, with the added problem of holding it with only three rifle companies. On New Year's Day (1 January 1942), the Bidor position was occupied and troops moved into bivouacs in their respective company areas. It was a good time to cook food and carry out long delayed administrative tasks. But, unexpectedly the situation changed rapidly on receipt of urgent reports that a Japanese Regiment was landing at Telok Ansan, to the rear of 12 Brigade's position. The Brigade (less 4/19 Hyderabad) moved to Telok Ansan to counter the new enemy threat. On 3 January, the Unit moved in vehicles and rejoined the Brigade at Telok Ansan. It took up its defence in depth of 5/2nd Punjab and A & SH.

Seasoned Japanese troops advanced rapidly down the Malayan peninsula.

There was a lot of enemy air activity, with reconnaissance aircraft scouting the Allied defensive positions, and invariably followed by bomber aircraft. On 3 January 1942, as the Unit was moving into its defences, an LMG deployed in anti-aircraft (AA) role, opened fire at a low flying Japanese reconnaissance aircraft. About an hour later, 'A' Company was heavily bombed by four enemy bombers, escorted by six fighter aircraft. Though numerous bombs exploded in close proximity of the trenches, only one OR was caught in the open and killed.

The day had seen a lot of enemy air activity with reconnaissance aircraft frequently scouting the Allied defensive positions, followed by bomber aircraft. After the air raids, it was reported the enemy had begun attacking areas north of Bidor. It was well known fact that if the Japanese managed to break through the defences, the artillery guns and transport fleet of 12 Infantry Brigade would be unable to reach the main road to Trolak, and they would be trapped and unable to provide further support to 12 Infantry Brigade.

Battle of Slim River (See Map 2)

As the Artillery guns and transport fleet were vital for providing further resistance to the advancing enemy, therefore, during the afternoon of 3 January, the Brigade withdrew further and began to occupy a new position north of Trolak. The new deployment comprised a 'one up' defensive position, with 4/19 Hyderabad Regt holding the 'outpost position', ahead of the other two units. The Battalion had reached Mile 60 during the night and it immediately began to prepare the new defensive position. To stop the advance of enemy tanks, a small bridge on the railway line was expeditiously demolished with explosive charges. The Battalion's defensive positions were in the midst of unusually thick jungle. Adjacent to the jungle was a large rubber estate, with a number of by-roads leading out from the main road. 5/2nd Punjab and A & SH were deployed in depth and they were able to put down some anti- tank mines.

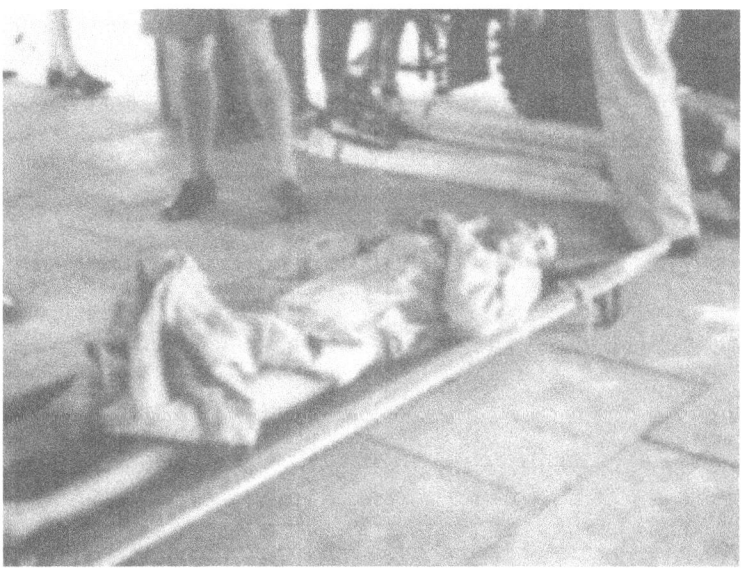

A wounded Japanese prisoner arrives in Singapore. He was one of the few Japanese soldiers to be taken prisoner during vicious fighting along the Malayan Peninsula.

Japanese troops crossing a jungle stream during their rapid advance through Malaya

On the morning of 5 January 1942, a visibly flustered Tamil plantation labourer came running through the lines and reported that Japanese troops, with nearly 100 heavy vehicles and tanks, were only about three miles away. Troops immediately occupied 'stand to' positions and readied their weapons. During the afternoon, about a company of Japanese soldiers was observed moving cautiously along the railway track. The well camouflaged troops of 'A' Company allowed enemy to advance till they were practically on the defensive wire obstacle, and then opened heavy fire. Automatic bursts of fire raked the surprised enemy, who jumped down on either side of the elevated railway embankment. The LMGs did a commendable job and tore large gaps in the enemy's ranks. The remaining enemy fled into the surrounding jungle, where they were engaged with high explosive (HE) 2-inch mortar bombs. The enemy suffered heavy casualties and over 150 dead bodies of Japanese soldiers were counted as they lay on either side of the railway embankment. After this fierce blow, the Japanese halted further advance and quickly withdrew north, back-tracking the way they had earlier advanced.

Once again, 'A' Company had been the first sub-unit to engage the enemy and it commenced a bitter engagement that would later be known as the famous 'Battle of Slim River'[2]. Next morning, patrols were sent into the jungle on flanks of the railway embankment, but no signs of the enemy were located. Around midnight, large numbers of the enemy were again heard, near 'A' Company's position on the railway line. It appeared the enemy had returned in strength to avenge their earlier losses. Clashes commenced as the enemy contacted patrols which had been deployed ahead of 'A' Company's defences, to cover the railway track and provide an early warning. At about 3 AM, the enemy contacted the Unit's defences in strength and also brought down intensive artillery fire. Troops in trenches could hear the loud rumble and clanking sounds of advancing tanks. In brilliant moonlight, the attackers moved down the main road with about 10 light tanks leading the advance. The light tanks were followed by about 20 armoured cars and a few medium tanks. Lastly, enemy infantry advanced close behind the medium tanks. The battle of 'Slim River' had begun in real earnest, with the well coordinated Japanese armour and infantry attack. 'B' Company was attacked by overpowering numbers of Japanese infantry. Along with Capt GK Mehta, the brave Company Commander, a platoon of 'A' Company ceased to exist. Remainder of the company withdrew to the main road to Trolak.

---

2 The Unit fought bravely and it would later win Battle Honour 'Slim River', for its valiant actions during the battle. The Battle of Slim River was however, decisively won by Japanese forces.

LONG TREK TO INDIA AND FREEDOM

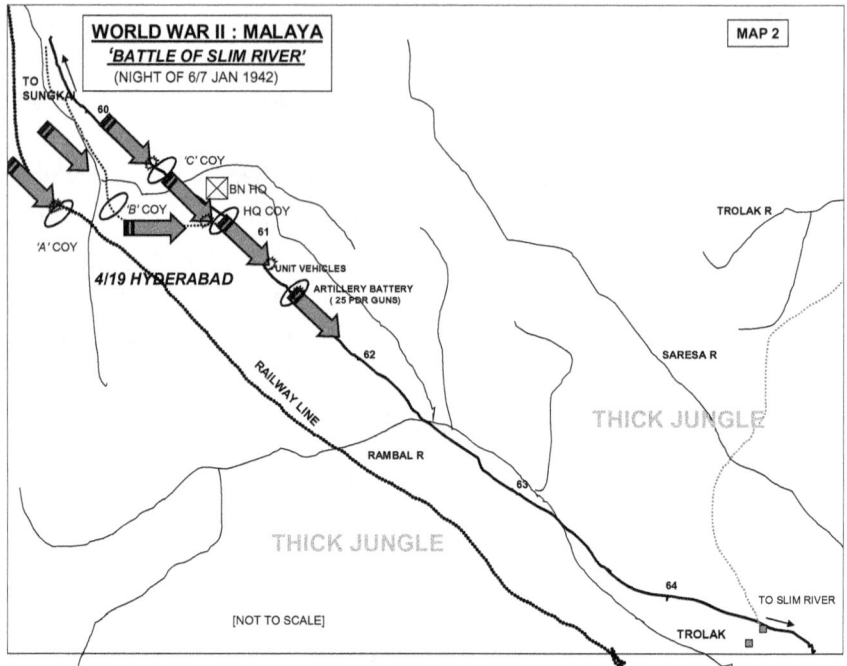

Battle of Slim River

Based on their previous night's experience, the enemy expected stiff opposition from the defenders. Therefore, the Japanese had launched an Infantry Division supported by armour, against 4/19 Hyderabad Regt and 12 Infantry Brigade. 'C' Company and then 'B' Company heard tank noises and reported the advance of enemy tanks and armoured vehicles. The only anti-tank weapon the troops possessed were improvised 'Molotov Cocktails'. Enemy infantry supported by the tanks, moved rapidly to isolate the forward defensive positions of the unit.

Japanese tanks, on the move

Shells from tank guns and MG fire blasted the defences and provided accurate support to the attacking Japanese infantry. In the darkness, the anti-tank gunners could manage to fire only two anti-tank rounds at the assaulting enemy tanks. However, both these rounds either missed their targets or were ineffective to halt the tanks. The anti-tank guns were destroyed by tank fire. The armour roared through the defensive positions, causing enormous destruction and casualties, in their wake. After the armour had passed through the position, the battered defenders rallied in small groups and continued to engage the on-rushing Japanese infantry. Though most of the telephone lines had been cut, isolated company groups kept up the bitter fight. There was a total lack of communications and passage of orders was disrupted. Enemy tanks broke through the Battalion's defences and succeeded in cutting up 5/2nd Punjab Regt and A & SH (both units were located in depth). The battle soon de-generated into a tactical nightmare and utter confusion prevailed. The inky darkness was punctuated by blinding flashes of exploding artillery shells. The sharp bangs of shells fired from tank main guns' and heavy rattle of tank MG fire, was mixed with the sounds of firing of small arms and loud shouts of Japanese and Indian soldiers. Heavy casualties were suffered by both sides during the savage fighting.

Lt K D Vasudeva

Capt Gopal Krishan Mehta

Lt KD Vasudeva, Transport Officer, received orders to move the Unit's vehicles to a safer location. He mounted a motor-cycle and rode off

Maj AD Brown, CO

to Battalion HQ, to confirm the order[3], and sadly he was never seen again. Meanwhile, Japanese tanks broke through to Battalion HQ of 4/19 Hyderabad Regt (killing Maj AD Brown, CO, and many more Unit's personnel). The tanks even blasted the units of 28 Infantry Brigade, which were deployed in the rear. A troop of anti-tank guns was wiped out before they could fire a single shot. A Gurkha Battalion was over-run and two batteries of 28 Infantry Brigade Artillery were totally destroyed. Fires raged everywhere, and by 9 AM the enemy tanks had destroyed a Light Anti Aircraft Battery that had tried to block their path. As the Japanese tanks were crossing a bridge near the gun position of 155 Field Regiment, the gunners gallantly resorted to direct firing of their 25 Pounder guns and managed to stop the leading tank, about 30 yards from their gun-position with a direct hit! However, fire from the following, enemy medium tanks that were following soon destroyed the artillery regiment. Tanks plunged forward to destroy targets in the rear areas.

Unable to stop the onrushing enemy tanks, remnants of both brigades were withdrawn across Slim River. There was only one surviving railway bridge across the river, which had been expeditiously repaired by Indian Engineers. The overall tactical situation soon became totally untenable, as Japanese infantry followed closely behind the rampaging tanks and destroyed positions of the Allied infantry. Surviving troops of the Unit formed isolated pockets of resistance and grimly fought to the end. After the Battle of Slim River, all that remained of 4/19 Hyderabad Regt were three officers and 180 men! Interestingly, during the battle, Capt GS Parab had been separated from the Unit. He luckily rejoined 4/19 Hyderabad Regt, after some interesting adventures[4].

---

3 Confirmation of the order was necessary, since in the past confusing orders had been received to move back the unit's transport. Later, these orders were countermanded and the vehicles had to be moved back. It is quite likely that Lt KD Vasudeva was killed by the onrushing enemy tanks.

4 An account of Parab's interesting evasion is given at Appendix 'B'.

Battle of Singapore (See Maps 3 & 4)

After the grim fighting at Slim River, remnants of 4/19 Hyderabad Regt were moved to Singapore Island, along with remainder of 12 Indian Infantry Brigade. At Singapore, the Unit was rested and re-equipped, while it prepared its defeces. A little later, some reinforcements arrived from 19 Hyderabad Regimental Centre, Agra, India. With the arrival of these fresh troops (and attachment of the remnants of 5/2nd Punjab), strength of the Unit rose to about 680 men. On 18 January 1942, the Battalion was ordered to prepare its defences on the north end of Singapore Island, overlooking the Causeway to Johore.

Since the Causeway was the only link with Malayan peninsula, its defence was considered vital, till all troops had been withdrawn from the mainland. On the morning of 31 January, troops who were preparing defensive positions along the northern, watched the blowing up of Causeway. It was an awesome sight. After the massive explosions water rushed through the 70 feet wide gap and Singapore Island was de-linked from the Malayan peninsula. 12 Infantry Brigade occupied defensive positions on Choa Chu-Klang Road. The Unit occupied its defences around Mile 11, while A & SH and 2/29th Australian Battalion, held the

Malay Peninsula (Johore) as seen from across the waterway, after the Causeway had been blown up on 31 January 1942.

forward positions. The Australian Battalion had replaced 5/2nd Punjab Regt, which had ceased to exist during Battle of Slim River. By 4 February 1942, Japanese heavy artillery had moved forward and deployed near the coast. Along with aerial bombings, Singapore was subjected to severe artillery bombardments. The enemy even raised an observation balloon at Johore, to view Allied Activity. At such times, a warning was sounded and troops rushed to their trenches as heavy artillery bombardments invariably followed. On the night of 8/9 February, heavy bombardments took place and Japanese armour and infantry landed on a 10 mile front, around Kranji. Powerful columns of enemy tanks and vehicles loaded with infantry moved into the island and rushed towards Singapore City.

Japanese Attacks On Singapore Island - Map 3

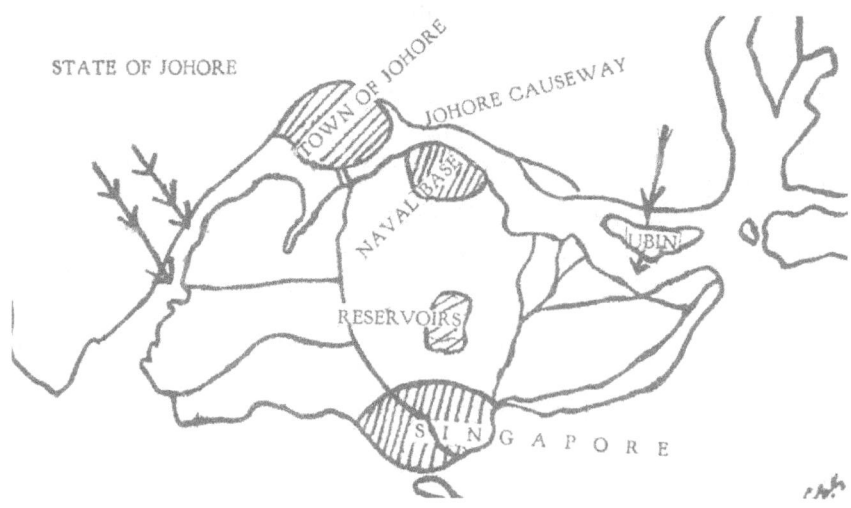

Allied troops kept up a bitter fight, and contested the Japanese advance. A force was even frantically assembled to counter-attack the Japanese! On 10 February, Japanese aircraft bombed the Battalion and explosions ripped through the area. Many oil barrels were hurled high in the air, before they exploded. The Unit suffered numerous casualties during the accurate air attacks. Shortly after dusk the enemy attacked in strength. Heavy fighting took place, and the Unit withdrew through the Australians to a position further down the road. Soon, a column of about 50 enemy tanks created a gap by smashing through the defences and headed towards Bukit Timah.

Japanese infantry began to pour through this gap in large numbers and complete confusion prevailed.

There was destruction all round and most places were in flames. Huge plumes of dark smoke rose into the sky and loud explosions were heard from Singapore City. By 12 February, remnants of the defenders had fallen back to outskirts of Singapore City, where a 'sea to sea perimeter' had been formed for the 'final battle'. In the hours that followed, bitter fighting took place along the perimeter and enemy tanks roared into Singapore City. There were repeated air attacks and massive artillery barrages landed on Singapore. At the final perimeter around Singapore City, the defenders tried their level best to hold off the Japanese thrusts. However, at most places the enemy columns broke through the perimeter and headed into the city's built-up areas.

JAPANESE LANDINGS - SINGAPORE   MAP 4

During this heavy fighting, both the defenders and civilians suffered heavy casualties. 4/19 Hyderabad Regt had suffered severely during the heavy artillery shelling and aerial bombing of Singapore

Island. The Units' Officers' Mess (including many priceless trophies) was destroyed in the heavy artillery fire and air attacks[5]*.

One of Singapore's 15-inch coastal defence guns, firing in an elevated position.

---

5 The priceless silver trophies that today adorn 4 Kumaon Officers' Mess, were rejected by the 'Board of Officers' at Secunderabad and left behind in the Unit's depot in India. These trophies were not considered 'good enough' to be taken by the Unit for its 'peace-tenure' in Singapore!

An Australian anti-tank gun faces Johore Bahru, from Singapore Island.

About 75,000 Indian soldiers were captured in Malaya/Singapore. Of these, about 20,000 joined Indian National Army (INA). Of those who refused to join INA, 11,000 died of malnutrition and atrocities in Japanese POW Camps and at the hands of prison guards. In the later fighting for 'freedom', for the next three years in Malaya and Burma, INA lost two officers and 150 Other Ranks (OR), killed in action. The INA's operations did not materially affect the formations of Indian Army (IA) or British Army, in any substantial manner. Nor did INA achieve any major victories that would dent the overall Allied 'war effort'. However INA remained a 'threat in being' and gave the British leadership sleepless nights, imagining the great negative effects it could cause, if there were to be another general uprising in Indian units/formations. Ghosts of *'Sepoy Mutiny of 1857'* troubled the British hierarchy endlessly and they dreaded losing India as a major support base, especially for operations in the east, against Japan.

Meanwhile, the Japanese used Singapore as a stepping stone, and continued their invasion to the south. A flotilla of ships passed through the Straits of Malacca and landed their troops on the large island of Sumatra. A number of refugees who had escaped before the invasion of Singapore, were rounded up in Sumatra and they were indeed treated very cruelly. Local inhabitants of the islands of Dutch East Indies, also faced the wrath and cruelty of the Japanese invaders. Advancing rapidly the Japanese spread rapidly inland and moved to the north. Advancing to Sumatra Island, they occupied Medan, before hopping islands to Java and its rich oil-fields (which were under Dutch control).

Thick, black smoke rises from Naval Base, Singapore

Japanese infantry on the move

Defenders in 'pill-boxes' at the water's edge at Singapore - February 1942

Fire-fighters battle flames caused by a Japanese air raid on Singapore Railway Station.

Boats with Japanese troops crossing Johor Straits from the mainland to Singapore

British troops surrendering to the Japanese in Singapore, on 15 February 1942.

At Medan, the invading Japanese troops behaved in a very cruel manner with the locals and small population of Sikhs, who had migrated from India and settled on the island. A notable figure among the Sikhs of Medan (Sumatra), was Capt Ranjit Singh (Royal Dutch Army) and founding member of English (medium) High School and Sikh temple (Gurudwara). He was treated harshly and tortured by the occupying Japanese forces. When the invading Japanese forces reached Medan, they were surprised to discover a fledgling Sikh community. True to their background, the Sikhs of Medan were an extremely tough and stubborn lot. The Sikhs refused to voluntarily bow down before the Japanese invaders. Thus, the Japanese were merciless and cracked down on the Sikhs and local inhabitants. Capt Ranjit Singh's son, Sardar Harcharan Singh was appointed *'Liaison Officer'* with 26 Indian Infantry Division, when it landed in Sumatra and reached Medan. Harcharan Singh was instrumental in identifying the Japanese personnel who were responsible for torturing the locals and Sikhs in Medan. With Harcharan Singh's efforts, these offending Japanese individuals were identified and appropriately punished by the British authorities.

Capt RANJIT SINGH (ROYAL DUTCH ARMY)

26 Indian Infantry Division arrives in Medan, Sumatra [S. Harcharan Singh (s/o Capt Ranjit Singh) was 'liaison officer' with 26 Indian Infantry Division. He is seated, second from right].

Sardar Harcharan Singh (extreme right) identifies Japanese military personnel who had carried out large scale torture of the population of Medan (Sumatra).

CHAPTER 2

CAPTIVITY AND ESCAPE

Victorious Japanese troops march through the streets of Singapore City

Prisoners-of-War (POW) in Singapore

For Fortress Singapore, the end came quickly. Around 7 PM on 14 February 1942, Singapore City fell to the Japanese and suddenly there was a great silence, after days of noisy small arms fire, artillery shelling and air raids. Thereafter, only random rifle shots were heard from various parts of Singapore. The Allied Commander, Lt Gen AE Percival signed an unconditional surrender on 15 February 1942, at '*Ford Factory*', and the

Singapore garrison of about 70,000 men passed into captivity as prisoner-of-war (POW). Remnants of 4/19 Hyderabad Regt had a little advantage of being taken captive near their pre-war barracks, in central Singapore. For next two nights after the capitulation, troops were told to remain in their trenches or dug-outs, from where they had been fighting the Japanese invaders. Officers of the unit had expected the prisoners to be shipped to faraway POW camps in Manchuria or Formosa (now Taiwan). But, they were pleasantly surprised to learn they were to be kept on Singapore Island, for the time being. After two days in trenches, the British, Australian and Indian prisoners were separated and taken to different POW camps.

Lt Gen Arthur Percival (second from right), walks to negotiate the capitulation of Allied forces at 'Ford Factory', Singapore, on 15 February 1942. It was the largest surrender of British led forces in history.

British & Australian troops were taken to Changi (located about 14 miles east of Singapore City) and placed in buildings, formerly housing a British battalion. Indians were generally sent to POW camps established in Nee Soon and Bidadari areas. Nee Soon was about nine miles north of Singapore City, on way to the Naval Base and dockyard. Formerly, it had been the location of Hong and Singapore Royal Artillery (HSRA). On 17 February, all weapons were collected by the Japanese captors. Asian officers and troops were marched to Farrar Park, where they were paraded in front of the main Pavilion. Prisoners had been permitted to take along only the clothing they wore and two day's food rations. Maj Iwaichi Fujiwara (Japanese Intelligence Officer) arrived at Farrar Park, accompanied by Capt Konishita (Japanese interpreter), Col Hunt (OC, 2nd Echlon), Col Niranjan Singh Gill (INA & ex 4/19 Hyderabad Regt), Capt Mohan Singh[1] (INA) and Giani Pritam Singh. All the prisoners were asked to stand up and a brief ceremony was performed. After the ceremony, Col Hunt marched up to Maj I Fujiwara and reported loudly in English, *'I hand over all Indian prisoners of war to the Japanese Govt'*. He then handed over some papers to Maj I Fujiwara, turned about and marched back.

---

1 Capt ('General') Mohan Singh (1909-1989) remains an enigmatic personality. His unit (1/14 Punjab Regt) was defeated at Jitra. After some days spent in the jungle, Mohan Singh and some others from the unit surrendered to Japanese, in a marsh. He was taken to Alor Starr and then made GOC of the First Indian National Army (INA), by the Japanese. Later, he fell out of favour with the Japanese, and was removed from INA and arrested. When Singapore was re-captured by Allied forces, Mohan Singh escaped to Medan in Sumatra. However, Medan had a small Sikh community that had been ill treated by the Japanese. Though a Sikh himself, Mohan Singh (who had been working with the Japanese), was not welcomed at Medan. So, he fled to interior areas and took shelter at a remote place called Siantar. Here, he remained in self-exile and finally gave himself up to conquering troops of 26 Infantry Division (Indian Army). After Independence, he entered 'public life' and served as Member of Parliament (Rajya Sabha).'General' Mohan Singh died at Jugiana village (Ludhiana) on 26 December 1989.

Prisoners-of-war at Singapore, await further instructions from their Japanese captors

Fujiwara then handed over the prisoners to Capt Mohan Singh. After Col Hunt had left, there were announcements over the loud-speakers in both English and Hindostani, asking the prisoners to remain seated. After the prisoners had sat down on the grass, they were addressed by Maj I Fujiwara, Capt Mohan Singh and lastly Giani Pritam Singh respectively. A gist of the addresses made at the Pavilion, are given in Appendix 'B'. After the addresses were over, all officers above the rank of Lieutenant (Lt) were invited to the Pavilion for a drink of Australian brandy. While the officers were having a neat drink of fiery, brandy, Maj Fujiwara invited them to discuss any matter they desired, with him. After the 'brandy drinking ceremony', officers of 4/19 Hyderabad Regt were told to proceed to Nee Soon POW Camp. By then the troops had already left the Pavillion grounds and proceeded to Nee Soon POW Camp, Singapore, along with some other units. The POW Camp was located at north-centre of Singapore Island. It comprised of a number of ageing barracks, built around a grassy quadrangular square – in happier times, this ground had often been used as a soccer pitch. The Camp was meant for 3000 men, but now it was to hold about 22,000 prisoners of war!

February 15, 1942 - British Surrender.
Lithograph print of a painting, by an unknown Japanese artist, of the signing of 'surrender documents' at Ford Factory, Bukit Timah. Gen. Yamashita (seated at centre, across table) thumps the table and emphasizes his terms for an 'unconditional surrender'.
[Lt.-Gen. Percival (above) consults with the officer to his left].

Over the next couple of days, the officers were addressed a number of times by Capt Mohan Singh and Maj Fujiwara. Capt Mohan Singh had been designated as General Officer Commanding (GOC), Indian National Army (INA) and 2 Lt Rattan Singh was his ADC. The GOC's staff comprised of personnel who had been promoted to the rank of officers. Mohan Singh told the officers in custody, to come and see him at anytime, and have frank discussions on any issue that may be bothering them. 'Gen' Mohan Singh's HQ was in the Singapore Police Barracks, located between Thompson Road and Bukit Timah Road, Singapore.

INA Badge

INA Badge

The Administrative Committee of Nee Soon POW Camp comprised of Indian officers who had joined INA, and they lived adjacent to Nee Soon Camp. The functions of Committee members were purely administrative in nature and creditably, they did not conduct any propaganda on the prisoners. The members functioned under Capt Mohan Singh, who remained in contact with the Japanese authorities.

'Kepell Harbour' was teeming with fleeing refugees, at the fall of Singapore

Captivity And Escape

Only Mohan Singh, M. Akram and some Japanese officers made attempts to 'brain-wash' the prisoners. They made repeated attempts to make the prisoners opt for INA. Administrative Committee members of INA, were as follows :-

1. Maj Kiani – 14 Punjab Regt.

2. Col NS Gill[2]* – 4/19 Hyderabad Regt.

3. Col Gilani – Indian State Force (Bahawalpur).

4. Col (Dr) Chatterjee – Indian Medical Service (IMS).

5. Capt Kashyap – 15 Field Coy. Madras Sappers & Miners.

6. Lt Col Bhonsle – Royal Garhwal Rifles.

7. Capt Munnawar Hussein – 4/19 Hyderabad Regt
(Assistant to Col NS Gill).

Col Niranjan Singh Gill was particularly active in improving the prisoner's conditions, since he wielded a lot of authority with the Japanese. On numerous occasions, he had obtained an immediate reprieve for some affected prisoners, by his personal intervention with Japanese authorities in Singapore. Gill would regularly lecture Indian officer-prisoners about the need to maintain discipline, the importance of saluting and need to live with honour & dignity. His interaction with the prisoners was responsible to make them come to terms with their changed status from proud soldiers

---

2 Col Niranjan Singh Gill had been educated in Prince of Wales Royal Indian Military College (PWRIMC, now called RIMC), Dehradun. A KCIO (he had graduated from Sandhurst, UK), he was commissioned in 7th Light Cavalry in September 1925. He later transferred to 4/19 Hyderabad Regt (now 4 Kumaon). A brilliant officer, Gill was among the first Indian officers to graduate from Staff College, Quetta, and was the first Indian officer to be posted at Army HQ, New Delhi, in 1939. When World War II broke out, Gill was among 'nine' Staff College qualified Indian officers serving in the Army. He was the senior-most officer to join Indian National Army (INA) as a founder member, with Mohan Singh, Shah Nawaz Khan and Gurdial Singh. He later fell out of favour with the Japanese and was imprisoned and made to undergo torturous 'solitary confinement'. After Second World War, he was tried by British along-with some senior officers of INA at Red Fort, Delhi. Later, in the 1960s he served as India's Ambassador to Panama and Thailand.

to lowly prisoners-of-war (POW). His frequent interactions with officer-prisoners and lectures to all prisoners achieved wonders in keeping up the unit's morale. However, at no time did Gill or any of the Administrative Committee members try to persuade Indian prisoners to become either Japanese stooges or to join INA. INA HQ did not exist in any camp where Indian prisoners were interned. In Singapore, INA themselves had a camp that was called, *'Volunteer's Camp'*. It consisted mainly of IA personnel who had been captured during fighting on mainland of Malaya. However despite all the efforts, Unit personnel remained disgusted by the sudden turn of events, during the campaign in Malaya. After heavy losses inflicted on the enemy, the men were surprised to see Japanese as their captors and masters. Despite the overwhelming odds, 4/19 Hyderabad Regt had shown great valour and fortitude during the heavy fighting in Malaya and Singapore[3]. In Singapore, there were seven POW Camps, where IA personnel were interned. The names of head of Administrative Committee of these POW Camps are as follows :-

(a) Seletar   - Lt Col Ushaq, [1st Hyderabad Infantry], Indian State Forces.

(b) Buller   - Maj Pharnavis, [4/19 Hyderabad Regt], he later moved to 'Fatigue Camp' on Bukit Timah Road

(c) Tengah Aerodrome - Maj Ghanshyam Singh[4], (Fatigue Camp) [3rd Cavalry]

(d) Kranji Camp   - (Not known).

(e) Nee Soon Camp - Maj Shah Nawaz Khan, [14th Punjab Regiment].

---

3 Although there was an overall allied defeat to Japanese forces in Malaya-Singapore Theatre, the Unit had fought with extreme gallantly. Thus, after the War ended, 4/19 Hyderabad Regt (now 4 Kumaon) was awarded two Battle Honours ['North Malaya' and 'Slim River'], for its brave actions.

4 Scion of a 'princely' family from Gujarat, Ghanshyam was serving in 3 Cavalry, and had been captured by the Japanese along-with his entire Regt. He was a great 'extrovert' and while in the POW Camp he quickly had a 'still' running, that liberally produced counterfeit alcohol! The 'good times' continued till he was caught by the Japanese. He was saved from a certain be-heading by fervent pleas of his brother-officers. Two officers of 3 Cavalry, Maj (later Lt Gen) Dhavalkar and Capt (later Maj Gen) HC Budhwar, underwent horrific times as POW. Later, both the officers were conferred with decoration of 'Member of British Empire' (MBE).

The over-crowded conditions in Nee Soon POW Camp were quite unbearable for the men. All prisoners had to sleep on the floor in barrack rooms, in four or five rows. The men were crammed in the barracks and there was no room even to stretch one's limbs. Due to heavy enemy bombardment, water pipes in the locality had burst and were rendered unusable. Thus, water had to be obtained from a small stream, near the camp. The stream's water was impure and it became a principal cause for the rapid spread of dysentery and other water-borne diseases. Japanese authorities were repeatedly requested to rectify the water supply system, but these requests were to no avail. After two weeks of complaining, some Sappers among the prisoners were employed to lay new pipes, and thankfully, the supply of piped water was resumed. However, the water supply was inadequate to quench all the men's thirst. The heat, humidity and severe working conditions, would sap the men's energy and add to their thirst. Latrine arrangements too, were grossly inadequate for such a large number of men. There was a perennial stench, filth and squalor because of inadequate latrine facilities. Flies increased rapidly and caused miserable conditions for the prisoners. Generally, there was rampant disease and ill health in the POW Camps.

There was no real shortage of medicines, as there had been plenty of medical supplies available before the city had capitulated. But, after the fall of Singapore, Japanese had taken hold of the medical stocks for use of their own sick and wounded troops, and shortages emerged for the prisoners. Three hospitals had been established at Nee Soon and medical officers (MOs) from among the prisoners were employed to care for their sick and wounded. However, the MOs were plagued by a constant shortage of medical stores. The Japanese authorities always maintained a callous attitude towards the medical care of prisoners. Repeated requests were made by representatives of prisoners, for an increase in medical supplies. One day, the Japanese Camp Commandant surprised everyone by sending a bouquet of flowers to each hospital, as a gesture of goodwill instead of badly needed medicines!

Care of prisoners who had been wounded during the Battle of Singapore was almost non-existent. Added to the need for medical care, was the ever increasing number of dysentery and malaria cases. The area had been heavily bombed before the Allies surrendered and there were innumerable craters in the soft soil. Sub-soil water and rain water, stood in these craters and mosquitoes bred in their thousands. The mosquitoes were a major menace and caused innumerable cases of malaria. Dysentery also spread quickly and despite the best efforts of MOs, the death rate among prisoners continued to rise. Congested living conditions and the free breeding of mosquitoes and flies, caused a rapid spread of the various diseases. MOs among the prisoners did their best with the limited stocks of medicines. They worked selflessly, provided urgently needed succor and saved the lives of many men. Although, prisoners were put to work in Camp Hospitals, there remained a great shortage of medical staff and medicines. The Civil Hospitals in Singapore had been taken over by the Japanese, for their own sick and wounded soldiers. Sick and wounded Allied personnel had been moved out of these hospitals and sent to POW Camps, where many died because of the lack of care and medicines.

Another factor that added to miserable conditions in the POW Camps was the rude and offensive behavior of Japanese guards. These guards had an indifferent attitude, and behaved in a rude and uncouth manner. Prisoners were tortured and beaten without ever being given reasons for their brutal treatment. Japanese personnel did not understand Allied badges of rank and on two occasions, VCOs of 11 Infantry Division Transport Company were physically beaten during fatigues, for failing to salute Japanese soldiers. On both these occasions, the concerned VCOs had to be hospitalized with severe injuries. When it was reported to senior Japanese officer at the Camp, he casually brushed aside the issue and insisted that beatings were necessary to maintain discipline amongst all soldiers. He added that beatings were regularly employed in the Japanese Army, and prisoners should not be unduly perturbed by this form of physical punishments!

Several cases occurred in the POW camps, where prisoners were bayoneted to death or beheaded by the guards. One such case occurred in Nee Soon POW Camp. A sepoy of Supply Corps was bayoneted to death for failing to salute a Japanese sentry. An order had been passed on the previous day, directing that all prisoners, including officers, were to salute Japanese sentries. The unfortunate Sepoy was unaware of the order and thus he lost his life! All civilians, including women, had to bow down low while they were passing any Japanese soldier. If they were riding a bicycle, they had to dismount and bow low, or they were humiliated and badly beaten on the spot. At times, even Malay civilians were bayoneted to death for flimsy reasons. These gory incidents were used by the Japanese to instil a measure of fear, in both the civilian population and prisoners in the POW Camps.

A Malay civilian is bayoneted to death, by Japanese soldiers.

There were shortages of food in all Japanese occupied territories. In particular, there were major shortages of sugar, flour, milk-powder and oil. Fresh milk was non-existent. In Nee Soon Camp, food for prisoners was prepared by Unit cooks in dark and dingy enclosures, which were known as *Camp Kitchens*. The cooks used provisions they received from the Camp Administrative Staff or other Japanese authorities. For the first three weeks, wheat flour (atta) was available and thus, '*rotis*' were cooked. Later, only rice was cooked in all POW Camps. Rations were limited and there was no arrangement for a supply of fresh vegetables or lentils. For all their meals, prisoners were given a watery gruel of rice. On some special days, such as the Japanese Emperor's Birthday, prisoners were delighted to see a few vegetable leaves floating in the swill! On rare occasions, watery lentils (*dal*) were provided along with the boiled rice. As per camp gossip, European prisoners in Changi POW Camp, sometimes even received tinned fish and meat! However, these rumours were short-lived, as it came to be known the basic diet in Changi POW Camp also comprised of the watery gruel of boiled rice, with an occasional smattering of vegetables. The fare at Changi was similar, if not worse to the food provided at POW Camps which held Indian prisoners.

Poor condition of European prisoners of war

There were great celebrations and cheer on the arrival of Red Cross packages, as the prisoners then received cigarettes, tea leaves, sugar and salt. However, there was never any milk or milk products, not even for the sick and wounded prisoners. Even for the occasional mug of tea, there was never any milk and rarely a lump of sugar. Rice provided to the prisoner's kitchens was of the poorest quality and would be teeming with insects and 'borers'. The European prisoners were not accustomed to either cooking or eating rice, thus, they often complained bitterly about the rice ration. Every morning before it was before dawn, the prisoners were ordered to assemble in the large playing field at the centre of Nee Soon POW Camp. The men were physically counted and a report was given to the senior

Japanese officer or senior Japanese NCO. Some prisoners were very weak with dysentery or malaria, but they had to be present at the assembly to be counted in the presence of Japanese authorities. Only the prisoners who were admitted in hospital, were allowed to be absent from the 'morning fall-in'. It was heart rending to see weak and sick prisoners collapse and lie on the ground, due to malnutrition and extreme exhaustion. The collapsed prisoners would remain lying on the ground for half an hour or more, till the prisoners were dispersed on fatigue details. Sadly, the prisoners were forbidden to speak or break ranks and help the colleagues who had collapsed!

The unit command structure had been kept intact. Troops were cared for by their Section and Platoon Commanders. The morale of prisoners from 'fighting arms' was generally good, however, some prisoners from 'Labour Corps' and Services, had deplorable 'march discipline'. These prisoners were a huge embarrassment to troops from 'Fighting Arms'. Australian prisoners were often heard singing loudly, as they marched for fatigue duties. For whatever reason, Japanese guards frowned upon Indian and Australian personnel from talking to one another. One day, an Australian column halted near a fatigue party from Nee Soon Camp. Japanese guards of both parties shook hands and were soon engaged in an animated discussion. Finding an opportune moment, Capt Balbir Singh cautiously approached the Australian column and asked a thin and ragged looking Australian prisoner about the conditions in their camp. The Australian soldier had winked and replied with a half smile, *'Things could be a lot worse. In any case, all this is not for long! Already the Americans have landed in Java. Cheerio Mate'*. Although the Australian soldier was ill informed about American troops landings in Java, his cheerful reply clearly summed up the positive attitude of Australians in the POW Camps of Singapore.

For the first few days, prisoners were employed to dig a massive trench around Nee Soon Camp, as a security obstacle. The Japanese had no intension of putting up a barbed wire fence around the large Camp. The trench was six feet wide, and it became more than six feet deep, once the excavated earth was thrown up on both the ends. This piled-up earth made the trench about ten feet deep. Some pools had formed at the bottom, where sub-soil water had risen to the surface. The trench was meant to deter the prisoners from escaping. However, due to frequent rains, sides of the trench would often collapse and had to be frequently repaired. Armed Japanese and INA sentries patrolled the outer edge of the trench in pairs. The sentries were rude and gruff, if any prisoner called out and tried to make conversation. Invariably, they would respond with threatening gestures or even point their rifles at the hapless prisoner. Prisoners who were not employed in digging of the trench, were sent on other fatigue duties, such as details to clean Singapore Town (the town was still in a filthy state), road repairing, and loading & unloading of railway trains at Singapore Railway Station[5].

During their first month in Nee Soon, the prisoners were subjected to frequent visits by high ranking Japanese officials. These inspections were a big strain, because the inspecting officers were never on time and prisoners had to fall-in and stand in the sun and rain for hours at a stretch, only to be told that the inspection would take place on the next day! When the inspecting officer arrived, many photographs were clicked, which the guards said were sent to Tokyo for publicity purposes.

There were practically no amenities for the prisoners in Nee Soon Camp. But, they were lucky to find a large stock of books, in an erstwhile Officers' Mess building of Hong Kong and Singapore Royal Artillery (HSRA). As the books were in English, the Japanese did not want them, and prisoners were permitted to use the books for their reading pleasure. Quite a few of the erstwhile British officer's bungalows were within the premises of POW Camp, and had been converted into accommodation for prisoners. Most of these bungalows had Wireless - Telephony (W/T) Sets, Refrigerators and other attractive electronic, items. When Japanese officers and troops came to know about the bungalows and their contents, there was a mad scramble for the attractive items, especially W/T sets. Once a Japanese officer came to a bungalow where there was a W/T set. During his rounds, he told a senior NCO (from 4/19 Hyderabad Regt) not to allow the W/T set to be taken by anybody else, as he wanted to take over the wireless equipment. After a couple of days, a Japanese NCO came to

---

5 These trips allowed the 'escapees' to get acquainted with the layout of Railway Station at Singapore.

the bungalow and demanded the W/T set. When the IA NCO told him that a Japanese officer had already appropriated it, the NCO threatened to beat him and forcibly took away the W/T set. When the officer returned and found the set missing, he was furious with the NCO and drew his sword to behead the poor man. With difficulty the scared NCO conveyed to the infuriated officer, that he could recognize the Japanese NCO, who had taken away the W/T set. That probably saved his life, as both the Indian NCO and Japanese officer then went to the Guard Room, where the culprit was pointed out. Thus, the IA NCO was saved from a gory end! However, the Japanese NCO always bore him a grudge, and would beat up the IA NCO during fatigue duty, on any flimsy excuse.

During March 1942, alarming reports were brought by groups of prisoners who had gone on 'fatigue' duties to Singapore city. It was reported that between mid February and early March 1942, the Japanese had carried out large scale massacres of Chinese population[6] in Singapore. It was basically the members of Chinese population, who were considered to be 'undesirable elements', that were eliminated. Most of these massacres were conducted at Changi Beach Park, Punggol Beach and on Sentosa Island (also called Pulau Blakang Matti). The estimated number of people who were massacred varies greatly, and was reported to be between 5000 and 100,000 Chinese. After news of these executions went around the prisoners, there was great fear whenever they were given threats of beheading and execution by firing squads.

There were several locations in Singapore, where the killings of Chinese took place. The most notable sites were at Changi Beach Park, Punggol Beach and Sentosa Island (Pulau Blakang Mati). About 300 to

---

6 The categories of 'undesirable' Chinese who were picked up for execution:-
  - Activists in the 'China Relief Fund'.
  - Wealthy men who had contributed generously to the Fund.
  - Members of 'Tan Kah Kee' or National Salvation Movement.
  - People from Hainan (perceived to be Communists).
  - 'China-born' Chinese who had come to Malaya after Second Sino-Japanese War.
  - Men with tattoos (believed to be members of 'Triad' or Chinese gangsters.
  - Chinese who had joined 'Singapore Overseas Chinese Anti-Japanese Volunteer Army.
  - Civil servants and British sympathizers.
  - Any Chinese individual who possessed arms.

400 Chinese were shot dead at Punggol Beach on 28 February 1942, by firing squad of the infamous Hojo Kemptai (Secret Military Police). The victims were some of the 1000 Chinese males who had been detained by the Japanese after a house-to-house search along Upper Serangoon Road. Several of these men had tattoos, which condemned them as members of Triad[7]. One of the most brutal killings took place at Changi Beach Park, on 20 February 1942. Sixty six Chinese males were lined up along the edge of the sea and shot by the Kemptai. The beach was the first of the killing sites of the Sook Ching massacre, with another one at Tanah Merah. Another site was Berhala Reping at Sentosa Beach (now Serapong Golf Course after land reclamation). In addition, surrendered British gunners awaiting Japanese internment buried some 300 bullet-ridden corpses that had washed up on the shore of Sentosa. These were corpses of civilians who had been transported from the docks at Tanjong Pagar, and were ruthlessly killed and tossed into the sea[8].

On 11 March 1942, the Camp Commandant of Nee Soon Camp ordered 500 men of 4/19 Hyderabad Regt to proceed to a new Camp, near Bukit Panjang Village. Capt Balbir Singh and Capt GS Parab accompanied these troops. The camp was located six miles from Nee Soon Camp. It was about four miles from a new runway being built at Tengha Airfield, and an adjoining stone quarry from where stone was excavated for the construction work. It was known as 'Fatigue Camp' on Bukit Timah (BT) Road. The prisoners were housed in old huts, which had been repaired by troops, after their arrival at 'Fatigue Camp'. Maj Ghanshyam Singh (3 Cavalry), was in-charge of 'Fatigue Camp', while Capt Balbir Singh was officer in-charge (OIC) of prisoners from 4/19 Hyderabad Regt.

Initially, the prisoners were marched every morning to a nearby stone quarry. Here, they broke rocks and loaded them in lorries for construction of the new runway, at Tengha Airfield. There was a fatigue party of about 4000 men already camping at the airfield, who would unload the

---

7 **Triad** refers to the many branches of Chinese groups of organized crime. Triad groups were based in countries that had a large Chinese population.

8 In a quarterly newsletter, the National Heritage Board of Singapore published the account of life story of a survivor named Chia Chew Soo whose father, uncles, aunts, brothers and sisters were bayoneted one after another, by Japanese soldiers in Simpang Village. This provides strong testimony that many killings by the Japanese were indiscriminate

vehicles and carry the rocks to the runway, under construction. A party of Australians was working in the quarry. They were made to carry the rocks and boulders about half a mile away, to another construction site. This location was at the geometric centre of Singapore Island and the Japanese ingeniously planned to construct an 80 meters tall monument, dedicated to their great victory over the Allies in Malaya and Singapore. A party of British prisoners was working at the site of the proposed monument. They were made to level the area and lay out a large garden.

Prisoners were often escorted to a Rubber Estate, located behind the POW Camp, to cut wood for the kitchens. Later, all prisoners of 4/19 Hyderabad Regt were put to work on the construction work taking place at Tengha Airfield. Here, the prisoners worked on the new runway and additional airport buildings. For construction work in Singapore, the engineers were Japanese while prisoners provided the entire labour force. Work was hard and prisoners were made to break stones and haul cement sacks needed for the construction work. The prisoner's lack of nourishment adversely affected their stamina, especially when they were made to toil for long hours in the hot and humid conditions. Indiscriminate floggings and humiliation by Japanese guards were a routine happening at the POW Camp, and made the prisoners' lives miserable. However, the threat of punishments did not dampen the prisoner's spirits and they would tell each other incredibly, humorous stories and make great plans for wonderful times they would have, once the War ended and they returned to their homes! They dearly remembered their loved ones in India and often imagined they were back at home, and partaking of delicious meals. They often dreamt of clean, comfortable beds and a carefree, sound sleep.

A Japanese officer (Lt Inova), with an interpreter, used to visit 'Fatigue Camp' and to oversee the work in progress. On one occasion, another Japanese officer came with him to ascertain whether work on the airfield's runway and buildings could be speeded up by increasing the size of labour force. Inova had been aghast when he learnt 'Fatigue Camp' did not have a fence or even a trench to restrain the prisoners from escaping. He must have taken immediate action, for a few days later, a platoon of Japanese Engineers arrived at the Camp and erected pre-fabricated cement pillars and unrolled a high, wire-mesh fence around the Camp. They also affixed search lights on tall, wooden pillars, at all ends of the boundary fence. The Japanese Engineers worked for about a week at 'Fatigue Camp', but no help was sought from prisoners, who continued their work at Tengah Airfield. The Japanese engineers worked diligently from sunrise till about an hour before sundown. Every two hours the Japanese would stop their work and take a 15 minutes break. During these breaks the Japanese would sit quietly on the ground and refrain from talking with one another. Even while they were working, the Japanese rarely talked to one another.

There were strict Camp Orders for prisoners to be within their huts, by sunset. Daily, at dusk, the search lights were switched '*on*' and their strong beams would sweep the fence, from end to end. If any prisoner was seen after sunset near the fence or was lit up by the search-light beams, there was likelihood of his being shot by the prison guards. Thus, all prisoners quickly moved indoors, within the prison huts, before it became dark. On one evening, despite a stern warning by the senior VCO, Sep Jiwan Singh of 'B' for Company, 4/19 Hyderabad Regt had ventured out of his barrack after dark. He was proceeding to another hut, when a loud rifle shot was heard. Next morning, during 'morning fall-in', Capt Balbir Singh was handed Sep Jiwan Singh's dead body, for further disposal. There was a clear bullet mark on Jiwan Singh's chest, where he had been shot by a guard. The unfortunate man's clothes were soaked with blood due to heavy bleeding, after receiving the bullet wound. On receiving the dead body, Balbir had asked the senior Japanese Camp NCO for permission to conduct last rites for the Indian soldier, and for firewood to conduct the cremation. Surprisingly, the Japanese NCO had laughed aloud and asked Balbir not to waste any firewood for this trifling matter. He had added, the soldier's body should be buried in a pit, without much ado, as the man had disobeyed Camp Rules and moved out of his barracks after sun-set! Quite aghast at what he had been told, Balbir had insisted that as per Indian traditions and IA orders, the dead body of a soldier of Hindu religion, had to be cremated. The Japanese NCO did not care much about Indian traditions, but he agreed the body had to be cremated, if orders said so! He told Balbir to get the necessary fire-wood from the prisoner's cook-house and carry out the cremation immediately. Thus, Sepoy Jiwan Singh's body was cremated near the Camp's perimeter fence, after getting wood from the cook-house. The incident of shooting dead the prisoner highlights the strictness with which Japanese rank and file followed their orders. It also shows the Japanese NCO's attitude, and how he readily agreed for the cremation, when told that orders called for a cremation – even though they were the orders of an enemy Army/Country.

Preparations for Escape

Two officers of the Battalion, Capt Balbir Singh[9]* and Capt Gangaram S Parab had failed to reconcile with their changed status as lowly prisoners. Thus, they had been planning to escape from the POW Camp and reach India, ever since the night of surrender. But, they had temporarily shelved the idea since everything was topsy-turvy and indiscriminate shooting was taking place. As there were only two officers of 4/19 Hyderabad Regt at 'Fatigue Camp', they felt their presence was essential for the welfare of their men. Also, since there were few officers in the POW Camp, they had to report frequently to the Japanese captors. It was felt their escape would be promptly discovered, leading to an easy re-capture, brutal punishments and even a horrible death.

Having heard of heavy fighting taking place in Burma, the officers reviewed their plans for returning overland to India. After lengthy discussions, Balbir and Parab hoped to get a boat or sampan and make for the nearest island and later, somehow reach India. However, they knew it was a dangerous plan, since the coast and harbour were known to be well guarded by the Japanese. Even if Balbir and Parab managed to procure a boat, they had little knowledge of handling a craft in the open sea. Thus, the plan to travel by sea was a non-starter. It was analyzed in detail and rejected.

By mid April 1942, Maj Pharnavis[10], Capt Dil Sukh Mann and Capt

---

9 While at Nee Soon POW Camp, Capt Balbir Singh was detailed to go to Singapore Railway Station with a working party to load a Japanese train with supplies for Penang. Whilst on the job, Balbir managed to smuggle a case of Australian Brandy. Six bottles were gifted to officers of the Unit while six bottles went to the VCOs. Needless to say, Balbir earned a 'shabash' and the officers and VCOs had a jolly good time, for the next few days. The fact that POW Camp guards could not detect smuggled goods moving into the Camp, had boosted everyone's morale and gave an impetus to plans for escape.

10 In 1944, he was tortured to death at a POW Camo in Singapore.

Ramaniah, RMO, with another 300 men from 4/19 Hyderabad Regt also moved to 'Fatigue Camp' on the Administrative Committee of Bidadari Camp. Lt Pritam Singh[11] had been severely wounded in the left shoulder, during an air raid on Singapore, and had been admitted in hospital at Singapore. On 15 February, after being discharged from hospital, he was sent to Bidadari Camp. Pritam had heard of the escape plans, and was eager to return to India. Balbir and Parab agreed to have Pritam with them in the escape and he was told accordingly, during a visit to Bidadari Camp.

Since there was an acute shortage of accommodation and food on Singapore Island, civilians were being allowed to return to their homes on the mainland, with permits issued by Japanese authorities. It was well known to Balbir, Parab and Pritam that their capture would mean brutal torture, which may be followed by certain death. Thus, in preparation for the escape all three officers changed their names and posed as clerks from a Rubber Estate. While on a fatigue duty in Singapore City, Balbir, Parab and Pritam succeeded in enrolling themselves as civilian members of 'India Independence League' (IIL). They obtained necessary travel permits and had false names endorsed on their IIL Cards as follows :-

(a) Balbir Singh   – Bhajan Singh [ex-clerk in Censor Office].

(b) GS Parab   – Prem Singh [sports dealer in Singapore].

(c) Pritam Singh – Balwant Singh [ex-clerk in Censor Office].

Since the prisoners were becoming physically weaker with each passing day due to dysentery, malaria and other diseases, it was decided to speed up the escape. Clothes, rations and money were secretly smuggled into the Camp. Although they were short of quinine and other drugs, Capt Ramaniah, RMO, arranged valuable medicines for the escape. Meanwhile, Pritam used the influence of his *'friends'* to get himself transferred to

---

11 Back in India, Pritam Singh commanded 1 Kumaon (Para), [now 3rd Battalion, Parachute Regt] Alongwith the Unit, Pritam proceeded to Poonch (over Hajipir Pass), and was besieged there for nearly one year. Pritam was promoted to Brig at Poonch, where he conducted the defensive battle in most professional and gallant manner, till link-up took place from Rajauri. Exploits of this gallant soldier are now folk lore in Poonch and his yellowed photograph still nostalgically adorns many a civilian home. He is very rightly known as 'Saviour of Poonch'.

Fatigue Camp on BT Road. Lt Balwant Singh [5/14th Punjab Regt] often expressed a keen desire to join in the escape. The matter was discussed in detail between Balbir, Parab and Pritam, and it was unanimously felt that Balwant could not be included, as four escapees would be easily discovered and apprehended. Thus, Balbir and the others felt it was far too dangerous, and Balwant was told he could not join the escapees. Lt Balwant Singh remained quite dejected for a long time[12].

Lt Pritam Singh while he was serving in 4/19 Hyderabad Regt

Lt Balwant Singh

Arrangements were made by Balbir, to obtain the inner material of a tent. This material was hand-stitched by the Unit tailor, into baggy shirts and trousers, for the three officers who were scheduled to escape. During the escape, Balbir wore the off-white shirt and baggy trousers, made from tough tent material, along with a whitish pugree and canvas, PT shoes. The escapees deliberately avoided khaki, which was a military colour and likely to disclose their identity as soldiers. To wear on his feet, Parab bought a pair of canvas, PT shoes, for one Straits Dollar. In addition, he found a large civilian hat with a wide brim, in the Royal Artillery barracks at Nee Soon Camp. The incongruous hat was useful for concealing an old

---

12 Along with a company of 5/14th Punjab Regt, Lt Balwant Singh was shipped from Singapore to a Labour Camp in the jungles of Borneo. Here, one day he was cruelly tied to a tree and bayoneted to death, for a minor infringement of camp rules. In later years, his widow would often castigate Balbir, for not permitting Balwant to join in their 'escape' to India.

piece of map they had salvaged from a bungalow near 'Fatigue Camp'. The piece of map was invaluable to the escapees, as it showed Malaya, Thailand, Burma and parts of eastern India, as well.

Money was urgently required for train tickets, travel permits, food and other expenses that were expected to be incurred during the escape. Cash was borrowed from some traders in Singapore and larger towns, on the way. There was little or no money with prisoners in both Nee Soon Camp and Fatigue Camp. However, one Sub Trilok Singh of 4/19 Hyderabad Regt, surprised them by lending a 'princely sum' of Rupees 60/-, which he had carefully hidden in a deep crack in the wall, at Fatigue Camp. The crack in the wall was not visible, as it had been cleverly sealed with clayey, mud. Some Indian traders in Singapore assisted them with money and valuable travel information. During work details to the city, both Balbir and Pritam had made friends with one Labh Singh, of a sports gear shop named 'Rose & Company' on North Bridge Road. He magnanimously loaned them 70 Straits Dollars. The money was collected by Balbir, through a friendly *watchman* at the railway crossing near Fatigue Camp. The Malay *watchman* was not aware of their 'escape plans'. He also inadvertently mentioned to Balbir that sale of rail tickets to the public, had commenced from 1 May 1942. Before that date, only military special trains and goods trains were functional. Climbing onto the open goods wagons was a rather difficult proposition for the prisoners, were weak with malnutrition and disease and getting weaker by the day.

'Straits Money' – *currency issued by Japanese Govt*

Balbir & Company' was another sports shop, located near *'Rose & Company'*. Before the War, the Unit had been buying sports equipment from both these firms. The owner of *Balbir & Company* used to frequently travel between Bangkok and Singapore, and he gave them valuable travel advice. In this manner, they managed to collect a fortune of 210 Straits Dollars and 60 Indian Rupees. During their time at 'Fatigue Camp', Balbir and Parab were able to maintain close contact with Nee Soon Camp, by making several visits to lodge complaints, about being neglected by the Medical Officer (MO). On the other hand they were extremely grateful to Capt Ramaniah, MO, who gave them a bonanza of a bottle each of valuable quinine tablets, water sterilizing tablets and some gauze bandages, for their journey.

Orders for move to Andaman Islands

There was another, worrying reason to hasten the escape. The prisoners had been told that a company of 4/19 Hyderabad Regt (with both Balbir and Parab) was soon to be shipped to an unknown destination. Unofficially, it was said these troops were being sent to either Java, Sumatra or Borneo for labour duties. Fortunately, this move of the company of 4/19 Hyderabad Regt was cancelled, and instead, 300 men of 5/14 Punjab Regt were sent to Borneo (along with Lt Balwant Singh). After a few days, orders were received for move of Balbir and Parab with 'B' Company, to Andaman Islands. Although no date had been given for the move, it was expected to take place during that very month. Thus, during his visit to 'Fatigue Camp', Niranjan Singh Gill[13] had been confidentially told by Balbir about their planned escape to India. In view of the impending escape, Gill was requested to have the move to Andaman

Col Niranjan Singh Gill

---

13 *Niranjan Singh Gill earned his education at RIMC, Dehradun. He was commissioned in 7 Light Cavalry Regiment, from Royal Military Academy, Sandhurst (UK), as a senior King's Commission Indian Officer (KCIO). Later, he transferred to 4/19 Hyderabad Regt (now 4 Kumaon). With an illustrious career unfolding, he was among the pioneer Indian officers to graduate from Staff College, Quetta (now in Pakistan) and the first Indian officer to be posted at Army HQ, New Delhi. Fired with a spirit of nationalism, in Singapore he joined INA as a founder-member. After Independence of India, Gill served as India's Ambassador to Mexico, Thailand and Panama.

Islands cancelled. However, Gill was uncertain whether Japanese plans could be changed at such short notice. Therefore, he suggested that the escape should be planned from Andaman Islands to India, by boat. However, Balbir told Gill that all efforts should be made to have the planned move to Andaman Islands cancelled, as it would be difficult to escape from Andaman Islands and travel across Andaman Sea and Bay of Bengal. They did not possess expertise to negotiate these seas, in a boat. Thus, a journey by boat would be disastrous. Gill agreed with Balbir's views and said he would try his best to convince the Japanese authorities to change their plans for move of the company.

Every day they waited expectantly for news of cancellation of their move to Andaman Islands. Ten days went by and no word was received from Gill. Meanwhile, the company received executive orders to set sail for Andaman Islands. On the next day, with a heavy heart Balbir and Parab lined up the troops of 'B' Company. The vehicles had been loaded earlier with their heavier kit. Now, the men awaited final orders to mount the vehicles and proceed to Singapore Harbour. At the harbour, they were to board a ship and set sail for Andaman Islands. Both officers were dejected as their plans for escape had been doomed to failure, even before the escape had been attempted. Just then, a Jeep careened into the Fatigue Camp at high speed, with Col NS Gill half standing in the co-driver's seat. Gill frantically waved his arms and shouted, *'Balbir, Balbir, your move has been cancelled. You are not to go to Andaman Islands!'* Gill's arrival was most providential and once again, the escape seemed to be a reality. The officers were elated and they happily ordered the men to unload the vehicles and move back to their huts.

The Escape

Though 'Fatigue Camp' was centrally located on Singapore Island, yet it was some distance away from Singapore Railway Station. In end of April, construction work at Tengah Airfield had been intensified and prisoners were taken daily in trucks to a nearby quarry, to break stones and load them in lorries. The loaded vehicles then moved to Tengah Airfield, where another group of prisoners would unload the stones. After cancellation of the move to Andaman Islands, there was great excitement and feverish preparations began for the escape to India. In consultation with other officers in the POW Camp, the date for escape was finalized as 4 May 1942. Maj Pharnavis (senior Indian officer in the POW Camp), promised to give Balbir, Parab and Pritam a clear head-start, by concealing the escape from Japanese for the first 24 hours. As a part of their final preparations for escape, a hole was surreptitiously cut in the Camp's new perimeter fence, and nicely concealed with boulders, sack-cloth and dry bushes. On the evening of 4 May 1942, the three officers wore clothes prepared for the escape and disguised themselves as refugees. Each officer carried a small bundle that contained a sheet, blanket, towel and some personal items.

Before dusk on 4 May 1942, the three officers were given a hearty meal, made from food supplies that had been smuggled into the POW Camp. A heart-rending parting took place with their comrades, including JCOs and men. After the touching farewell, all three officers silently left the barracks and moved close to the fence. They were aware that after dark, no movement was permitted outside the barracks. If they were caught by the guards, they would be severely punished. On being caught under suspicious circumstances and fully geared for an escape, they could even be summarily shot or beheaded! Carrying their bundles, the three escapees cautiously moved forward in the dark. On nearing the fence they lay down, well concealed in a small hollow in the ground, they had reconnoitered earlier. After confirming there were no Japanese or INA guards in the vicinity, Balbir sprinted forward and quickly removed the boulders and bushes from the hole that they had earlier cut in the wire-fence. He got on his hands and knees and carefully slipped through the concealed hole in the wire fence. Once on the other side, he lay prone and unmoving. Balbir could feel his heart thumping loudly, with excitement.

After dusk on 4 May 1942, avoiding the search-light beam Balbir sprinted to the hole in the wire-fence and crawled to the other side. Then, Parab and Pritam followed him across the fence.

He looked around him to make sure he had not been seen by Camp guards. Then, he raised his hand and signalled to the others to move across the fence. On seeing Balbir's hand signal, the others knew it was safe to cross the fence. So, one by one, Parab followed by Pritam, crawled through the hole in the wire and joined Balbir across the fence. Once they were on the other side of the fence, they lay still and looked about to see if there was any activity from the Camp sentries. After confirming the

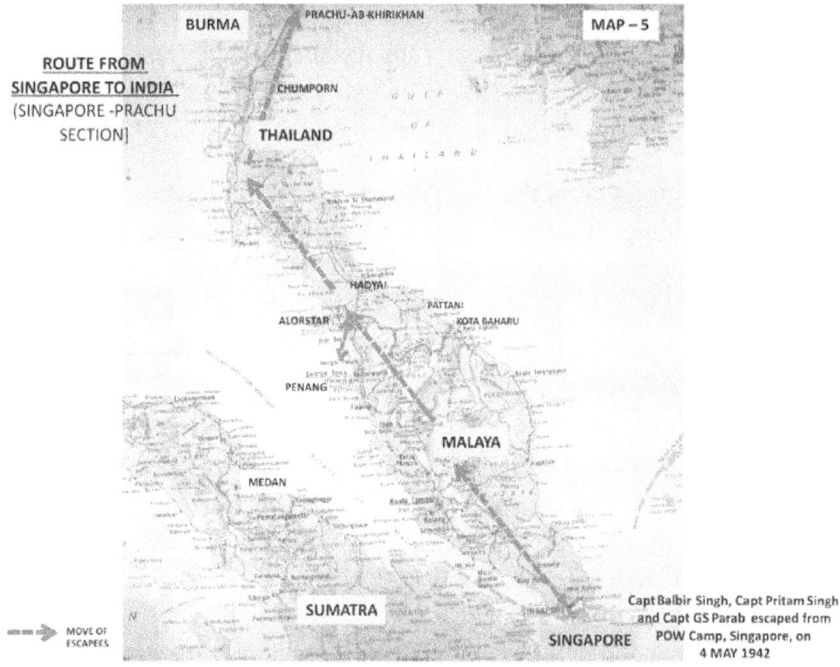

guards had not seen them, the three escapees carefully rose to their feet and proceeded in the dark towards Bukit Timah Road. They moved quickly, but remained in the shadows, carefully avoiding all lights. Luckily, there were no vehicles plying on the road and they were not seen by anyone. They began walking towards Singapore Railway Station, keeping on the grass lining of the road. They were alert and ready to ready to jump into the surrounding bushes, if a vehicle were to be seen. It was a long walk and the escapees gained their confidence as they silently trudged along the dark and deserted roads of Singapore. At North Bridge Road, they came across the tram line. Building up courage, the trio went and sat in a deserted tram station.

Soon, a well lit tram rumbled into the tram station and screeched to a halt. They jumped up from the seat and nonchalantly boarded the tram. Once inside the tram, they sat on yellow painted, wooden seats. The only other passenger was an old, Malay man, who kept looking at his brown, canvas duffel bag. The conductor was a middle aged Chinese, wearing a blue cotton coat. He shuffled up to them and raised his eyebrows. They confidently bought tickets to Singapore Railway Station and sat back to enjoy their newly found freedom. The Singapore streets were dark and deserted, and many familiar shop signs flashed past the tram's windows. They got off at the Railway Station, which was well lit and a number of armed Japanese soldiers could be seen moving about in small groups.

After alighting from the tram, the trio waited for a while in shadows near the tram-lines. Finally, they mustered up enough courage to walk confidently into Singapore Railway Station. Parab and Pritam felt rather uncomfortable, as they were sitting on a bench that was directly below a bright electric light, while Balbir walked towards the Booking Office. Some Japanese soldiers could be seen conversing jovially, and no INA guards could be seen anywhere near the Railway Station. An armed Japanese soldier paced up and down the platform. He periodically sauntered to the Booking Office, before turning back and returning the way he had come. A number of Malays, with a sprinkling of Sikhs and Tamils, were waiting on the platform to board the train.

Thankfully, no-one paid attention to the three officers, who were wearing atrocious looking clothing, made of roughly stitched, tent inners. Balbir stood behind the bench for a while, and then walked confidently to the ticket counter. He moved forward after the armed Japanese guard had turned his back to him, and was pacing the other way. Balbir easily purchased three train tickets to Prai, with help of the IIL Cards. Each ticket to Prai cost 10 Straits Dollars. After Balbir had paid a fortune of 30 Straits Dollars, the sleepy Malay Ticket Clerk suddenly livened and asked for the other two persons who were to travel to Prai. Balbir was initially taken aback, but he satisfied the inquisitive clerk by pointing to the bench on which Parab and Pritam were dozing peacefully. The clerk spoke in rough Malay, and looked rather surprised to hear good, cultured English being spoken by such a slovenly dressed refugee! However, the clerk quickly prepared three tickets and handed them to Balbir, who heaved a sigh of relief. The clerk then busied himself with examining the money he had received and counted the currency notes over and over again.

After purchasing tickets, the trio felt more confident and spent the remainder night on the wooden bench. To avoid attracting attention, they sat in one place and conversed in low whispers. They deliberately avoided walking around the platform, as there were numerous detachments of

Captivity And Escape

Japanese soldiers sitting at different places. In the morning, they boarded a train going north, which was already packed with people. the crowded compartment, they sat well apart to avoid detection. Pritam sat next to a burly Sikh with a bandaged arm, who was traveling to Alorstar. A wood - burning, steam engine hauled the train across the repaired causeway and through heavily forested and picturesque countryside of Malaya. For the next day and night, the escapees sat quietly in the swaying railway compartment, lost in thought. They were excited as their great journey had finally begun. For the moment, the joys of having successfully escaped from the POW Camp in Singapore blocked out fears of re-capture and anxieties of the long journey that lay ahead. The rhythmic, clickety-clack sound of the train's wheels induced a deep slumber and within a short while of leaving Singapore, all three officers were dozing fitfully in the swaying railway compartment. During the train journey they were neither questioned nor harmed in any way. Only the ticket inspectors occasionally moved among the passengers and asked them to show their tickets. The escapees saw parties of armed Japanese soldiers standing on platforms at many stations as the train rattled and chugged its way to the north.

During afternoon of 6 May, the train pulled into Prai. Here, Balbir got off and bought onward tickets for Alorstar. They traveled in the same train and at about 7 PM they reached Alorstar, near the border with Thailand. On the train, Pritam had been talking to a Sikh, PWD Engineer, named Dogar Singh. Pritam had asked him location of the Gurudwara at Alorstar. Dogar Singh[14] had said he planned to stay at the Gurudwara and would take them along with him, after they reached the railway station at Alorstar. On learning of Dogar Singh's background from Pritam, the three escapees put their heads together and decided not to go along with the individual. Thus, when the train got to Alorstar the escapees politely thanked Dogar Singh, picked up their ragged bundles and walked out of the Railway Station. Without talking to anyone or asking for directions they headed out of the darkened township. Soon, they had hidden themselves in the deep jungles that surrounded Alorstar.

---

14 During his conversation, Pritam had discovered that Dogar Singh had been a PWD engineer, who was removed from his job by the British for some misdeeds. Later, he had been reinstated by the Japanese. Although, Dogar Singh had not been told about the escape, his background had dissuaded the officers from using the Gurudwara at Alorstar, for fears of being recaptured.

CHAPTER 3

'GREEN HELL' (THAILAND TO BURMA)

Crossing into Thailand

To their great disappointment, they were told that despite 'war-time' removal of some travel restrictions, it was still necessary to have valid passports to be able to cross the border into Thailand. In addition, these passports were required to be stamped with endorsements, by the Japanese Occupation Authorities! After a few nights in their hide-out, the escapees realized the health hazards of staying any longer in the jungle. The mosquito and other insect bites were getting most troublesome. They would have to move through the jungle and attempt an early border crossing. So, they approached a Border Crossing Point and hid in the nearby undergrowth. From their hide, they carefully observed the Border Crossing and saw it was well guarded by armed Japanese soldiers. The Thai guards on the other side seemed to have good relations with the Japanese Military Police. They did not make the crossing, as they were certain to be caught on the Thai side and handed back to the Japanese, with disastrous consequences. Thus, they hid for a number of days, unsuccessfully trying to find a way to cross into Thailand. Swarms of mosquitoes made their lives miserable and there was the constant threat of contracting malaria. To make matters worse, the escapees neither possessed passports and nor did they have financial means to acquire passports from the authorities. Meanwhile, their supplies were running out and they had reached the end of their patience. Thus, they decided to immediately attempt a border crossing.

On 19 May, they finally made an attempt to get across the border. At about 11 AM, as they were moving forward to cross the IB, they heard urgent shouts from the Japanese Border Post, behind them. Instead of turning back, they speeded up and broke into a run. However, the sharp cracks of rifle fire halted them in their tracks. The bullets snapped over their heads and dropped a shower of leaves on the escapees. They immediately stopped and turned around with raised hands. Angry members of a Japanese patrol quickly caught up with them and a fuming soldier cuffed Parab on his head. Parab fell to the ground, but with an acrobatic twist he managed to hang on to his outlandish hat. After landing on the ground, with a deft move Parab extracted the precious map and pushed it into the front of his shirt. The three officers were roughly herded back to the Border Check Post at Padang Besar. Feigning ignorance about location of the IB, they were lucky to be released after being given a sound beating. During their brief stay in custody of Japanese Border Guards, they were rudely searched and their precious stock of quinine and water sterilizing tablets was confiscated. This was a serious setback as malaria and dysentery were rampant and they could ill afford to fall sick during the escape.

After the close call with border guards, once again they hid in the jungle near the IB. This time, they remained hidden in the jungle for more than a fortnight. Bites from teeming mosquitoes and repulsive leeches made their lives extremely miserable. As they were woefully short of food and water, the escapees knew they had to move on, if they wanted to avoid being recaptured. In extreme desperation Pritam recalled that Dogar Singh had mentioned they could easily obtain passports in Penang and have them stamped by the Japanese authorities. As they had been unable to cross the IB and enter Thailand, they decided to go to Penang and get the necessary travel documents. That evening they emerged from their jungle hide-out and boarded a train to Penang. Alighting from the train at Penang, they cautiously went to a Government Office, near the jetty. Here, they met a rotund, Sikh clerk, who listened to them most sympathetically and told them to come back on the next day. They stayed overnight in the Gurudwara along with many other people. While talking to others, they discovered that most people were making money on the sly, by doing illegal trade in smuggling sugar from Malaya to Thailand! They went back the next day and found the Sikh clerk to be most helpful. They had themselves photographed and through the clerk's generous efforts, they managed to obtain the necessary 'travel passes'. The passes were valid for three months, and it was endorsed on them, they had to urgently visit their relatives in Bangkok (Thailand).

While they were in Penang, Balbir was recognized by a Sepoy of 4/19 Hyderabad Regt. The man was running a shop and he told them, a VCO of the Unit named Sub Diwan Singh, was in the local INA Camp. They went to the INA Camp and met with the VCO. Diwan Singh had escaped from Fatigue Camp, BT Road, Singapore, about a fortnight earlier than them, but he had been unable to cross the IB to Thailand. They offered to take Diwan Singh with them, but surprisingly he seemed to have reconciled to his fate and refused their genuine offer. He stayed on in Penang, and it is not known what became of him. They also met with two officers [2 Lt Mathur (RIASC) & 2 Lt Trilokekar (RIASC)] and a jawan [Sep Risal Singh] of IA. Having obtained passes, they happily returned to Alorstar and again hid in the jungle. On the next day, they went to the Gurudwara and contacted Dogar Singh, who took their passes to a Japanese officer, to be stamped. When they returned the next day to collect the documents, Dogar Singh gave them bad news of an altercation between Japanese and Thai authorities. As a result of this disagreement, Thai Border Authorities were refusing to accept passes issued by the Japanese. Dogar Singh further informed them, that for crossing the IB and travel in Thailand, they would now require Thai passports, in addition to the Japanese papers. They were terribly disappointed and felt the efforts they had made, had all come to naught. The three escaped officers were a dejected lot and extremely annoyed with Dogar Singh, for not informing them earlier, of the changed circumstances. They felt the trip to Penang had been a worthless exercise and a complete waste of time, effort and money!

With little hope of legally getting across the IB, they were willing to take a calculated risk and illegally cross the IB into Thailand. During one of their visits to Alorstar town, the officers learnt of a Sikh farmer named Ujagar Singh, who frequently crossed to Thailand with a loaded bullock cart. He supposedly knew the guards well, on both sides of the border. After carefully finding Ujagar's whereabouts, they gingerly approached the Sikh farmer. He readily agreed to take them across the IB, but for a fair sum of money. As a seasoned entrepreneur, Ujagar wanted more than half the money in advance. Although they had nagging doubts about the farmer's integrity, in their desperate condition the escapees had no choice but to believe him. So they decided to take the risk, and they pooled-in their meager monetary resources. They paid the advance and finalized the place and time, they would meet Ujagar Singh on 22 May. A positive development was that Dogar Singh had vouched for the farmer's integrity and also given them a letters of introduction, addressed to other friends in Thailand.

After they had decided to cross the IB illegally. On 21 May, Balbir and Parab cautiously made a trip to Padang Besar. They were very careful after their earlier, unpleasant experience of being caught by the Japanese. They quickly found a vendor, who changed some of their money to Thai currency. After exchanging the currency, they were pleased with themselves and quickly returned to their now familiar jungle hide-out. The next day, 22 May 1942, was a big day for the escapees. They left their hideout early and met Ujagar Singh with his bullock cart, at the pre-designated time and spot, near the border. Ujagar Singh made them lie in the bullock cart and carefully covered them carefully with loose hay. He warned them not to talk or move till he told them they were across the border. He then cracked a small whip and the bullock cart jerked forward, its wooden wheels creaking loudly. Ujagar Singh walked on one side of the cart, and lying hidden in the hay, the escapees had many anxious moments. They literally froze, when they heard the loud voices of Japanese guards at the border crossing. The three escapees lay unmoving beneath the hay, knowing they had no chance to escaping if the guards decided to prod the hay with long bayonets on their rifles, and conduct a detailed search. Luckily, the guards joked with Ujagar Singh and conducted only a random search, and did not prod the hay with the bayonets on their rifles.

The escapees lay unmoving under the hay and their doubts about the farmer's integrity eased when they heard him joke, first with Japanese and then Thai Border Guards. *'Bandeyoh, chhipe raho teh hilo nahi'* he said loudly to them in chaste Punjabi, as he took the bullock cart safely across the IB. Once the cart was well hidden in the jungle on the Thai side, the relieved officers emerged from the hay and happily jumped to the ground. Removing strands of hay from their clothes, they profusely thanked the smiling farmer and paid him the remainder amount of money. They picked up their bundles and quickly disappeared into the jungle. The three were delighted to be in Thailand, which was supposedly 'free' and not directly under Japanese occupation.

Dogar Singh had warned them, that Thai Customs officials often carried out surprise check of documents of passengers, on trains running between Konge and Hadyai. He had said 210 tikals were required for a Thai passport. However, the passport could be got only after someone had stood surety for them. They could neither find someone to stand surety for them and nor did they have enough money to get the necessary passports from Thai Immigration authorities. Thus, they had no option but to risk traveling in Thailand, without the necessary documents. To avoid the checking of documents being done on trains, they decided to walk to Hadyai. After a long walk on wooden sleepers between the rail tracks, they cautiously entered Hadyai Railway Station. It was around midnight and fortunately there were no people to be seen on the platform They decided to pass remainder of the night sitting on wooden benches on the platform. However, on scanning the railway platform they were scared to see about 30 Japanese soldiers sitting together on the platform, with their rifles placed in upright stacks. On seeing the Japanese, the escapees separated and individually bought rail tickets to travel from Hadyai to Prachu-ab-Khirikan (located further to the north.).

They dozed while they sat on different wooden benches, on the platform. In the morning, they boarded a train heading to Bangkok. Not wanting to attract undue attention, they sat in different compartments. It was a big relief for them, when the train finally pulled out of Hadyai. Hauled by its 'wood-burning' steam engine, the train chugged northwards, along the narrow, Thai peninsula. They passed numerous small stations like Bandoh, Chumporn and others. They were glad to be safely seated in the moving train, when they clattered past Chumporn and saw a large group of about 60 enemy soldiers sitting on the platform. The Japanese soldiers were apparently waiting for a train. On 27 May, they reached the small, coastal town called Prachu-ab-Khirikan, located on the east coast of the narrow Thai peninsula.

Jungle Crossing to Burma

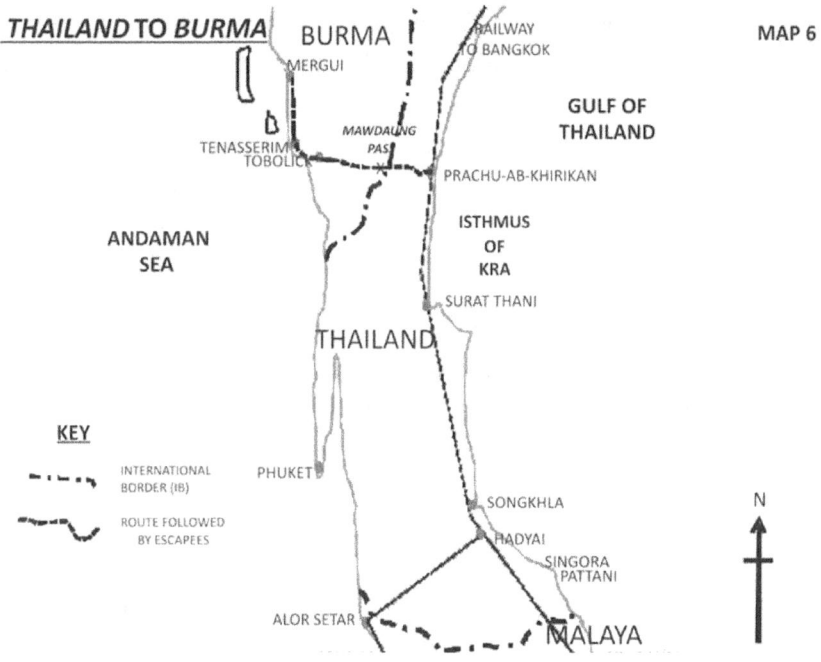

They alighted cautiously from the train, as there were many Japanese soldiers camping on large piece of flat ground, in front of the Railway Station. Also, there were a number of Japanese soldiers walking about on the platform. As they were leaving the Railway Station, an aircraft flew low and thundered over the town. Instinctively, all three officers dived for cover, but they promptly stood up and roared with laughter. They had forgotten they were in neutral Thailand and the aircraft sound they had just heard was probably a Royal Thailand Air Force plane, on a routine sortie!

At Prachu-ab-Khirikan they asked a seemingly affluent Thai for the whereabouts of anyone from India. When they were told there was only one man from India, they immediately went to meet him. He turned out to be a benevolent, Pathan named Khan Zaman, who had married a Thai girl and owned a meat shop in town. He possessed a number of cattle, which the escapees learnt he periodically acquired from cattle smugglers. The Pathan and his wife lived outside the town and willingly agreed to shelter the trio. The couple had a playful little daughter, who was fascinated by the three strange looking travelers[1]. They talked of North-West Frontier region & Punjab, and gained Zaman's confidence. Hesitantly, the Pathan opened-up and began to disclose his colourful past. He told them he had murdered a man near Peshawar, in his younger days, and was wanted by British authorities. To avoid being arrested, Khan Zaman had fled to Calcutta and then moved to Burma. From Burma, he had come to this remote Thai town, as a fugitive. He now had a meat shop, but mainly earned his livelihood by smuggling cattle to and from Burma – an occupation in which he was well versed!

When the escapees informed Khan Zaman they needed to travel to Burma and India, he told them about some hidden jungle trails that crossed inhospitable terrain and led to Burma. Zaman assured them confidently that they would never be apprehended on the hidden trails he was recommending for their journey to Burma. He, however, warned them that traversing nearly 100 miles in the jungles was a formidable task, even in good weather conditions. He said the jungle crossing would be a nightmare in monsoon rains. He told them, the first day's march would take them to a small village at the edge of deep jungle. Beyond the village lay thick, forbidding jungles, crossing of which would be the most difficult part of their journey. As monsoon rains had begun to lash the area, Khan Zaman urged them not to follow the jungle trails to Burma. As he knew the area well, he insisted that it would be a suicidal venture in rainy weather.

Faced with difficult options, the escapees sat down and reviewed their future plans. Khan Zaman had even offered them the option of staying on at Prachu and working with him. He said they could easily be married and settle down to a nice life in Prachu. Zaman assured them cattle smuggling was a fairly lucrative business and assured them, soon they would be rich

---

1 Nearly 47 years later, in 1989, Balbir returned to Singapore and retraced his journey along the escape route. He met and thanked most of the people (or their descendants), who had assisted in the escape. At Prachu-ab-Kirikhan, he was saddened to learn that both Zaman and his Thai wife had passed away. However, he met their daughter and they joyfully recounted the old times. The daughter (now a middle aged woman), told Balbir that it had been rumoured they were captured in the jungle and shot by the Japanese. She was happy to learn that they had all reached India safely. They had then celebrated over dinner.

men. Considering the uncertain times, it was a tempting offer. However, their status as IA officers and the burning desire to reach India made them politely decline Zaman's offer. They told him, they were willing to face the risks of moving along difficult jungle trails, even in monsoon rains if they could get to India. With a heavy heart, the crusty old Pathan allowed them to leave his home and proceed with their plans. Zaman's kindly Thai wife wrapped a small bundle of food for their journey and Zaman even sent his servant-boy named 'Kaka' and another Thai young man, to guide them on their way. After tearful farewells, they left Khan Zaman and followed the two servant boys. The small group of five individuals walked the whole day over meandering paths. As the sun was going down, they neared a village nestling in the foothills, and at the edge of the jungle. Kaka and the Thai young man spoke to the village elders in front of a large thatched hut. After animated discussions, the group was taken upstairs and made comfortable for the night. They were even given a hot meal of rice, lentils and deep fried tubers. When the villagers had left, Kaka chuckled and told them, the village elders had been impressed when they were told the three escapees were accomplices of Khan Zaman and very accomplished cattle lifters. They were now proceeding to Burma along the jungle route to bring back a large, herd of stolen cattle!

Next morning before leaving the village, the escapees were questioned by the villagers about their plans to return with the herd of cattle. Since they had already been told by Kaka, they could easily convince the over-awed villagers about their expertise in cattle lifting and future plans of soon returning with the large herd of cattle, they planned to steal in Burma. Cunningly, Pritam convinced the Village elders that as they had been so well treated, they would leave two heads of cattle at the village. With difficulty, they controlled their laughter at the great respect they suddenly seemed to have earned. After an elaborate farewell, the three escapees followed Kaka and the young Thai to the nearby foothills. Though Kaka had boasted about his knowledge of the route to Burma, he could not lead them to the proper track! But as he had been living with Khan Zaman and taking cattle for grazing, Kaka had some knowledge of the area. He soon found the entry point, beyond which lay the jungle route to Burma. Pointing to the large break in trees, Kaka and his companion said their hurried goodbyes and returned to Prachu and Khan Zaman.

Monsoon rains had set in and leeches and mosquitoes turned the trek into a terrible nightmare. The danger of wild animals and merciless dacoits added to their woes. The old Pathan's description of the perilous route could not have been more accurate. The escapees often wondered if they had made the right decision to follow the jungle route. During this part of the journey they encountered the most difficult conditions, they had ever experienced in their lives. The only thing that kept their spirits up was the fact that they were heading towards India and there was no turning back! So, with sheer grit and determination, the tired and famished officers plodded on in incessant rains and often lost their way in the thick jungle[2]. Initially, a group of inquisitive monkeys had followed them on their way. The monkeys would swing overhead from tall branches and they chattered shrilly. When the escapees entered the dark and silent primary jungle where sun's rays never entered, the monkeys had turned back and did not accompany the escapees any further.

The stench of rotting wood continually assailed their noses, as they trudged through the dark jungle. Although they never spoke out aloud, each officer was aware of the grave dangers that lurked ahead. The torrential monsoon downpours made movement difficult and at times they could barely see one another through the heavy mist. They lost a track of time and could not recollect the day or date. However, they marched on and remained determined as ever to succeed in finally reaching India. Having taken the decision to move by the jungle route, they vowed to either reach Burma or perish in the deep jungle!

In this manner they trudged on through the forbidding jungles. When they halted for the night, Balbir would collect firewood and help Parab with the cooking of rice and lentils. Pritam would scout around and find a safe spot for the night. He would build a small shelter with branches and bundles of leaves that had been pulled off from the surrounding trees.

---

[2] To overcome their fears and fatigue, they would loudly sing a song as they trudged deeper into the silent and deep jungle. Words of the song in Hindustani are, 'Chal, chal re naujawan, door tera gaon, aur thake paon. Rukna tera kaam nahin, chalna teri shaan. Chal, chal re naujawan ...'. The song spurred them on and they could forget about their travails for a while.

Some of the dense jungles traversed by the escapees in monsoon rains.

Invariably, heavy rains would leave them soaked to the skin and it was difficult to find dry firewood for their cooking fire. As they lay down to sleep, invariably in wet clothes, swarms of ants and other jungle insects would crawl over their bodies and cover them with a multitude of painful bites.

On the second day after leaving the village, as they began to cook their evening meal they were suddenly surrounded by some mean looking bandits. Six or seven bandits stood around them, while another two or three men lurked in the dark shadows. The bandits were herding about 20 heads of cattle. Their clothing was drenched in rain and appeared to be of a dark colour. The bandits had dirty scarves tied tightly around their heads, and they wielded nasty looking *dahs* and large knives. The trio were lined up against the large trees and bodily searched in a rough and rude manner. Initially, the cattle-lifting bandits took away the escapees' medicines, but later threw them down in disgust, as they could neither read the labels which were in English, nor decipher their usage. Loud words and fingers placed on their lips, spelt solemn warnings for the trio to remain silent and not to make a sound. After giving the warnings, the cattle lifters departed as silently as they had arrived. Alongwith the stolen cattle, the bandits headed towards the village. The escapees were shaken by the incident and knew they were fortunate to have survived. They vowed to be more careful in future, and decided Pritam would be positioned as a 'look-out', while Balbir and Parab cooked the evening meal.

On the third day after leaving the village, the track went up some heavily jungled hills and crossed over a Pass. At the Pass they saw a number of marks made on the trees, with dahs. They quickly crossed the Pass and descended on the other side. Going by what Khan Zaman had told them, the Pass was located on the IB. Thus, they had crossed over to Burma. The mountain Pass was called Mawduang Pass. After crossing the Mawduang Pass, they went down a steep track. Recent rains had made the track slippery and it was difficult to find stable foot-holds. In the valley below they were going across a fast flowing mountain stream when the three of them were swept away by the raging torrent. They could barely keep their heads above the turbulent, muddy waters. After floundering in the torrent for a while, they somehow managed to survive by desperately clinging to roots that protruded from the sheer mud-banks. However, all their belongings, including the precious quinine tablets, were washed away in the rapid flow. Soaked to the skin and panting from exhaustion, they helped each other to safety atop the slippery bank. They were tired, terrified and all hope suddenly seemed to be lost.

After a good rest they recovered their strength and spirits, to resume the onward trek. After walking for about an hour, the trio realized they were repeatedly passing the same landmarks. They had a strong suspicion they were going round in circles and could be lost in the forbidding jungle. In their weary state, they continued to hack their way over steep slopes and along overgrown and unfamiliar tracks, but their fears continued to grow.as they passed some marks they had made on a tree-trunk. Soon, it was confirmed they had been going round in circles and were surely lost in the dense jungle. In their exhausted state, the situation seemed utterly hopeless. They had long run out of the provisions that Khan Zaman's kindly wife had provided for them. Weakened by starvation, they were on the verge of collapse. They were plagued with hallucinations and began to harbour visions of a sad and lonely end, deep in the deep jungles of

Thailand/Burma. In their terrible state, they even contemplated suicide to end the endless misery. However, on the fifth day of their hopeless plight they were sitting silently, huddled in the dense undergrowth, when the most incredible thing happened. They heard unfamiliar sounds of dogs barking and a cock crowing. They stared at one another in utter disbelief, as these were the sounds of human habitation!

At first, they thought their ears were playing tricks in their exhausted state. But when they sat still and listened carefully, above the constant hum of jungle insects they could even hear the excited shouts of children playing. With great joy they realized that the sounds were indeed real and not a figment of their weary imagination. It was too good to be true and seemed like a gift from heaven. With renewed energy they followed the sounds and soon staggered into a small jungle clearing, with a couple of thatched huts. Half naked children shrieked in amazement and ran back to their mothers, as the three unkempt strangers broke from the jungle and entered the clearing. Dogs barked wildly and soon the villagers had gathered to watch the three strangers, who had collapsed from their exhaustion. There was a silence as villagers stared at the three fugitives who appeared to have walked in from another world.

Conversing in sign-language, the simple tribals warmly welcomed the escapees and offered them a sumptuous meal of hot rice, delicious yams with sweet, ripe bananas. It was a lavish treat after their frugal life in the jungle. They warmly thanked their hosts and after eating, they slept fitfully in one of the huts. The good food and rest suitably revived the three officers. Next morning, inquisitive children overcame their fears and came to sit with the escapees. They were fascinated by the officer's beards and some children even ventured to touch their faces. The escapees wanted to stay longer in the welcome surroundings of the jungle village and rest their weary bodies, but the harsh reality of their status as escaped prisoners forced them to continue with their journey. They did not want these friendly villagers to face the wrath of Japanese Army for helping the escapees. They warmly thanked the hospitable villagers and walked into the thick jungle. Before leaving the village, Balbir gave the excited children a peacock feather he had been carrying in his pocket ever since they had left Mantien. He told them in Hindustani, the feather would bring them luck. He doubted whether they understood him, but the eldest boy shyly stepped forward and took the feather in his hand. The other children clapped happily and ventured to touch the feather with their fingers.

Some days later, on 5 June 1942, and again in a state of utter exhaustion, they limped into the outskirts of a small township located on the jungle-edge, named Tabolick. Exhausted and hungry, they tiredly thumped each other on the back as they were proud to have reached habitation in Burma. It was truly wonderful to be alive. Wide smiles cracked their tired faces, as they sank to the ground and inhaled the wonderful smell of damp grass. However, their problems were far from over. They still had a long way to travel. Also, Burma was on the front lines and heavy fighting was raging between Allies and Japanese forces. Due to proximity of the front-lines, Japanese troops were extremely alert and present in larger numbers. The escapees realized they would have to be more careful in Burma. But, for the moment, the pleasing feeling of having reached Burma, blocked out all their fears of the future. The primary needs of hunger and sleep were so overpowering that nothing else seemed to matter!

The trio knew they had overcome the Pathan's predictions of doom, and literally achieved the impossible by crossing to Burma during Monsoon rains. They had hacked their way through more than 100 miles of forbidding jungles in eight days, braving torrential monsoon downpours! It was a tremendous feat of human endurance, even for physically fit and well nourished soldiers. However, the feat had been accomplished by escapees, who were in a ragged physical and mental condition. They had succeeded because of their dogged determination and the burning desire to reach India. At Tabolick they came upon a derelict tin mine called *'Tabolick Tin Dredging Company'*. Since they were now a long way off from Malaya, Balbir, Pritam and Parab decided it was time to change their identity as 'Clerk', 'Store-man' and 'Overseer' respectively, of the Tin Mine. From Tabolick they went by country boat to Mergui via Tenasserim.

On the country boat from Tabolik, they sat on temporary seats made of wooden planks. The boat took them down the muddy river and suddenly the foliage along the river banks ended and the area opened up to the vast blue waters of the sea. On reaching the open sea, the boat hugged the jagged coast and rolled precariously with each wave, causing passengers to be quite sick. A middle aged, and educated Indian was sitting between Balbir and Pritam. After brief introductions, he asked them if they were members of IIL. When they replied in the negative, he started up a lively conversation. He told them he worked in a store in Bangkok and was on his way to Mergui, to check on the plight of his wife and her parents after the Japanese invasion. He had not been home since the Japanese had occupied Burma. Balbir asked him about the conditions in Thailand. He said, at the beginning of the war Govt of Thailand had not treated Indians well. But, through the mediation of Swami Satya Nand, matters had improved and now there were lesser restrictions imposed on Indians. After looking around to ascertain that he was not being overheard by others, he said softly, *'The Thais are already tired of Japanese interference in their affairs. The Japanese want everything to be done in their way, without reference to Thailand authorities. The Thais have to remain silent for fear of repercussions from Japanese military forces, who maintain an indirect control over the Govt'.*

Referring to the recent air crash in which Swami Satya Nand, Giani Pritam Singh and Capt Akram Khan of INA had reportedly been killed, he said it was suspected by both Indians and Thai authorities, the air crash had been engineered by Japanese to get rid of these prominent Indians. It had been done because the Japanese did not like Satya Nand's 'straight talking'. The Thai Prime Minister had great regards for the Swami and he had wept when he had learnt of the air crash. It was said the Thai Prime Minister had not been in favour of the Swami's going to Japan. He would have surely stopped him, if Swami had planned to leave from Bangkok. But he had been powerless, as the group had flown out from Singapore. He said a cultural relationship existed between Thailand & India, and the Swami had done valuable work for Govt of Thailand. He had added, Indians in Thailand thought of Swami as being rather outspoken. He had apparently seen through Japanese designs and talked straight while discussing the issue of India's Independence. This was the main reason, why he was not popular with Japanese, and they had wanted to get rid of him. The feeling among Indians was that Japanese were only concerned with conquering India. The Japnese concerns about India's Independence were quite a farce. The Indian gentleman's eyes shone with emotion, and he had looked around to see that he had not been heard by others on the boat. However, as the boat entered the sea, suddenly the gentleman became very silent and his face turned an ashen colour. He staggered to the side of the heaving boat and retched uncontrollably into the sea, every time the boat rose up on a wave and came down suddenly. Between waves, he solemnly shook his head and advised his newly found friends, that they must desist from eating a heavy breakfast, if they wanted to ever take a boat trip into the sea!

On disembarking at Mergui, they were questioned by a suspicious Burma Police Officer, who had a couple of Police Constables with him. As planned, they passed themselves off as employees of 'Tabolick Tin Dredging Company'. However, the Police Officer's suspicions seemed to grow, as he knew the particular Tin Mine was a derelict and was not functional. However, Balbir handled the tense situation splendidly, and stated confidently that the Mine was to re-start its operations from July onwards, with new staff members. However, the Police Officer was not convinced and asked them to get someone to vouch for what they had just told him. Not knowing what to do, the escapees confidently walked towards the nearby market- place, with the Burma Police Officer and Constables following closely behind them.

Luckily, they found a provision shop run by an Indian, at the very beginning of the market. They quickly entered the store and Balbir quickly told the astounded shop owner in Hindustani about their status as IA officers. They prayed the man understood 'Hindustani', or all would be lost. Seeing the shopkeeper nod his head, Balbir added they had told the Police Officer a concocted story of their working at Tabolick Tin Mine, and requested him to vouch for their good character. Speedily following the escapees, the Police Officer and his men also entered the shop. The shop owner smiled and told the Police Officer something in rapid Burmese, causing the policemen to laugh. The three escapees simply stood beside the Indian shop-keeper and smiled innocently. The Police Officer scowled and said something to the shop owner in Burmese. The shop owner made a longish speech to the Police Officer and repeatedly pointed towards the escapees. At the end of the speech, the Police Officer swung around and left the shop in a huff, followed by the Police Constables.

After the Police Officer had departed, the shop-owner smiled and told them his name was Prem Chand, and his grandfather had migrated from Punjab in India. With a smile he added his family spoke Hindostani at home. He added that he had just given the policemen a guarantee for the three of them, as men of good character. He said they were very fortunate to have run into him, as there were only a few people in the area who had a good knowledge of Hindostani. He added with a smile, the Police Officer had told him he was from Tabolick and knew the Tin Mine was a derelict! However, Prem Chand had convinced him the Mine was very soon going to resume its operations. Prem Chand then offered them a cup of hot tea, and told them how to travel to Tazvoy. He warned them to be extremely careful, as dangerous dacoits infested the area. He also told them he had heard there were Australian prisoners in Mergui, Ye and Tavoy. While at Mergui, they had noticed that a bulk of traders and shop-keepers appeared to be extremely scared of the Japanese. They asked Prem Chand the reasons for this strange behavior, and. were told that whenever Japanese required labour, they rounded up the shopkeepers. The Japanese had often brutally assaulted the traders and asked them to pay money, if they could not do the labour work. The escapees thanked Prem Chand profusely and left his shop, feeling very grateful they had not been captured by the Burma Police Officer, who was working for the Japanese.

After leaving Prem Chand's shop they quickly proceeded to the jetty. On the way they saw many ragged Burmese soldiers straggling in the streets. The Burmese seemed to be running their own government, but under Japanese supervision. They were glad to move out from Mergui, and on 15 June, they traveled by launch, boat and bus. To reach Tavoy during the evening of 16 June. At Tavoy, they walked through dark streets, to the Gurudwara. They found the Gurudwara packed with refugees, who were squatting on the ground and some were asleep on the first floor. After the Japanese occupation, it appeared that many people had decided to stay on in Tavoy. They planned to proceed to Rangoon or Pegu, after travel conditions had improved. The refugees told the escapees that the area between Tavoy and Moulmein was infested with merciless dacoits, who were very hostile, even during the best of times. However, with uncertainties of war-time, the dacoits were expected to be even more dangerous. The area was close to the border with Thailand and therefore, it was somewhat of a 'no-man's land'. Some well-wishers among the refugees dissuaded the escapees from going any further along this route to the north, without forming a larger group for their security. When they asked people in the Gurudwara whether any of them were going to the north, they were told no one wanted to go along that route, till it had been declared safe for travel. So, the three escapees held a serious discussion and weighed their chances. After debating the problem in detail, they finally took a bold decision to take the risk and travel north, on their own, by the same route!

The Government of lower Burma belonged to 'Thakin Party', that had been established by Japanese. The Party was anti Indian and a number of checks had been enforced on movement of Indians. The escapees learnt that Indian passengers were required to obtain a pass before they could buy train or bus tickets to leave Tavoy. Despite their lack of '*travel passes*', on the next day they boarded a crowded bus proceeding to Yeh. They asked for tickets to Yeh, but were told to show *travel passes,* which unfortunately they did not possess. But, the bus conductor was a considerate man and he permitted them to sit in the bus. However, he told them the bus would be going to the Police Station for some routine work, and they could obtain the 'travel passes' and then purchase the necessary tickets. The bus started up and made a stop at the Police Station. All passengers were herded off the bus and taken inside the Police Station, for some 'checking' by the Japanese authorities. Inside the Police Station, a rotund, bespectacled Japanese officer and his Interpreter sat at a large table. When the escapees turn came, they went into the room and the Interpreter asked for their names, profession, reasons for going to Rangoon and duration of their stay in Rangoon. They confidently told the Interpreter they worked with 'Tabolick Tin Dredging Company' and were proceeding to Rangoon to meet their relatives. They added, they were worried about their relatives, because of the ongoing war and required passes to buy the bus tickets. Their replies were translated by the Interpreter, and the Japanese officer nodded and seemed satisfied. They were asked to wait for five minutes and then given the necessary permits to leave Tavoy. Bowing low and profusely thanking the Japanese officer, they left his office. Once outside, they jumped with joy and were thankful for the good luck. They quickly boarded the bus, and confidently bought bus tickets after proudly brandishing the newly obtained *'travel passes'*. The Conductor smiled condescendingly and gave them three tickets for travel to Yeh. Shortly after the bus had left Tavoy, it crossed two river ferries. At each ferry site, they were alarmed to see a detachment of Japanese soldiers who were bodily searching all travelers. Luckily, their bus was not stopped at the ferries. The road was well paved and the bus moved with a good speed. They reached Yeh during the evening of 18 June, after an uneventful bus journey.

They stayed at the local Gurudwara in Yeh. There was a railway line from Yeh to Moulmein, but trains were not plying on it as a bridge had been destroyed during the fighting. Therefore, on the morning of 19 June, they set off from Yeh on foot and walked for 22 miles along the railway track to Lamaing. This part of their journey was rather tough as they had to walk on jagged stones of the rail track. Torn canvas shoes and painful blisters on the feet, added to their misery in great measure. Hostile people lived near the railway track, and they were a constant menace. A village on that section of the railway track was known to be particularly dangerous. They had been warned at Yeh, to stay away from the hostile people of this village. They could not forget the horrified looks on faces of some refugees from south India, when they had recollected their tragic story! The refugees had described their sorry plight, when they were waylaid between Yeh and Moulmein. The refugee group had been robbed and two of its members were murdered by bandits from the hostile village.

As they walked along the railway line, the trio could literally feel the animosity of the villagers. The villagers sat in front of their huts, along the railway line and stared at the trio, as they went past the village. The three officers speedily moved along the railway line, without either looking at the villagers or stopping to talk with them. The trio relied on speed and they did not give the villagers any time to organize themselves to harass the escapees. Though it was extremely painful, the trio increased their speed by taking long steps on the stony surface and even broke into a run, after they had passed the village. In great pain from their badly bruised feet, they staggered into Lamaing, in the dark. They stayed the night in

Lamaing and left the next day, by train.

They had had enough of walking for a while, and the relief of sitting in a train compartment was truly unimaginable. They sat in the swaying railway carriage, very thankful they were not walking on sharp stones. Through the windows they were delighted to get a glimpse of the beautiful, blue-green waters of Andaman Sea. It was a heady feeling to know the shores of India lay across those cool waters. However, their joy was dampened, by thoughts of the long and tricky journey that lay ahead, across unknown territories that were under Japanese occupation. Most of the bridges were built on thick, wooden supports and trains went over them with a loud, and hollow clattering sound. The escapees continued by train and reached Moulmein on 24 June 1942. On the way they saw numerous Japanese military trains flash past at high speeds, both during day and at night. The trains were loaded with troops, vehicles, military equipment and once they even saw some horses. The Japanese military trains moved at high speeds, and were all proceeding towards Rangoon and beyond.

At Moulmein, Capt Parab developed a high fever, leaving his two companions very worried, as they thought he was sick with malarial fever! It was decided by Balbir and Pritam that Parab must immediately get some good medical treatment. Therefore, despite the great risks involved, Parab was admitted in the Convent Hospital, run by Eurasian and European nuns. In Moulmein city, they sensed an overpowering feeling of fear, from Japanese authorities. On making subtle enquiries, an Indian shopkeeper told them that some large and small shopkeepers had been jailed for two days and made to undergo hard labour. This was because they had been discounting the value of 10 cent notes in annas and pice. While Parab was in hospital, once again Balbir and Pritam stayed in a local gurudwara. They were pleased to learn from the medical nurses that Parab's fever had not been caused by malaria, and he would be discharged from hospital in a few days time. Their money had almost run out and they had to urgently organize some more cash, to be able to continue with their journey. So, they approached one Arjan Singh, a wealthy shop owner and wood contractor, who even owned a few elephants. However, they were shocked when Arjan Singh reached into his pocket and offered Rs 5/- ! They felt totally humiliated and declined to take his money. At the Gurudwara, they had met four Sikh youth named Shyam Singh, Santokh Singh, Jagbir Singh and Bhag Singh, all belonging to 8th Burma Rifles. The four individuals had been living as civilians, ever since their unit had disintegrated, after clashing with advancing Japanese forces. They told the escapees that treatment of POWs in Moulmein was quite pathetic. The four Sikhs, and a civilian (of Indian origin) wanted to go to India. They had some money, so, the escapees agreed to include them in their group. Due to shortage of money, the escapees were going through a difficult period. For many days now, their food comprised of only rice and salt and they were dressed in rags. Their large group of seven individuals left Moulmein on 30 June by ferry-boat, and arrived at Martaban.

On the ferry-boat they encountered four stragglers from 8 Gurkha Rifles. The Gurkha soldiers were silent and subdued, but seemed glad to be in the company of IA officers. They proceeded together by rail, bus, ferry-boat, on foot along rail tracks and by cycle rickshaws to Pegu via Thaton. In this manner, they arrived in Pegu on 2 July. The bridge over Sittang River had been destroyed in the fighting, and all movement across the river was being conducted in country boats. The stretch of railway line between Thaton and Bilin was patrolled by armed policemen on a trolley, to ward off belligerent dacoits that infested the area. The escapees stayed in Pegu for two days and moved on to Rangoon.

As they walked into Rangoon on 4 July 1942, a flight of Allied bombers droned over the city in broad daylight. Japanese MG and AA fire could be heard from the city, number of its buildings were reduced to rubble. After making two or three bombing runs, the aircraft droned away from the deserted city. Thereafter, only a few locals and Japanese troops were visible. The group of 8 GR and Burma Rifles soldiers, with whom they had been travelling from Pegu, decided not to continue to India. Break-up of the group, left the escapees in a dire financial crisis, and they moved to the Gurudwara in Rangoon. However, they found 30 – 40 people staying at the Gurudwara, many of whom appeared to be of a suspicious nature. Suspecting that Japanese agents were present in the Gurudwara, they approached one Gurdit Singh, Gurudwara Chairman and Member of IIL, and told him they had to leave urgently because of their pressing business interests in the city. Gurdit Singh had appeared friendly and he had examined the IIL Cards which they had been issued at Singapore. He told them to obtain fresh IIL Cards from the local IIL Office, as they would not be able to buy rail tickets with their present IIL Cards. Gurdit Singh had even offered to obtain some employment for them in Rangoon, but, they had politely refused his magnanimous offer.

Despite Gurdit Singh's protests, they moved to another Gurudwara on Manigaon- Prome Road, which was located about 3 miles outside Rangoon. From Manigaon, the escapees twice went back into Rangoon and visited the IIL Office. The three escapees again joined IIL by paying Rs 1/- each. The fresh member-ship of IIL enabled them to purchase railway tickets, after a recommendation had been made to the Station Master. While at IIL Office, Rangoon, they heard news and propaganda that a resurgent INA that numbered 70, 000 to 90, 000 men, would soon gain total victory, as it marched into India. While returning after the second visit, Balbir came across a Japanese staff car parked on a street corner. An Indian-looking driver was standing next to the car and he hailed Balbir in Hindustani. When Balbir stopped next to him, the driver told him with a smile, that he had earlier been a Sep in IA and now he was driver of a Japanese officer. He surprised Balbir by asking him whether he had been in Singapore! Balbir felt the Sep may have recognized him, so he feigned a coughing bout, mumbled incoherently and rapidly walked away from the Japanese car and its inquisitive, Indian driver.

Back at the Gurudwara they met an amicable Sindhi merchant, who they felt could be taken into confidence, and he also appeared to have plenty of money. They told him how their financial problems were restricting travel to India. The Sindhi merchant appeared to be a die-hard nationalist. He said he understood their problems and voluntarily gave them Rs 200/-. This windfall temporarily removed their financial woes. At the Gurudwara they also met an ex Sub-Inspector of Police, named Pritam Singh, who lived at Monywa. He disheartened them, by saying he had repeatedly tried to get back to India, but each time he had failed, because of the 'papers' that were required. When he could not get back to India, Pritam Singh began to conduct trade between Rangoon and Monywa. He knew Monywa well and promised to accompany the escapees, to his 'home-town', as he called Monywa! He also told them, a 'Business Pass' was needed to conduct any kind of trade in Burma. He added, the Pass would be useful during their further travels. Thus when they had agreed, the well meaning and helpful Indian helped them obtain 'Business Passes' with their new IIL Membership Cards.

However, despite the IIL membership and recommendations for Station Master to sell them rail tickets, it was only with a great amount of difficulty they could purchase train tickets from Rangoon to Mandalay. On 9 August, they left the Gurudwara at Manigaon and walked to Rangoon Railway Station, and boarded the evening train to Mandalay. Pritam Singh (of Monywa) accompanied them on this journey by train. The Gorkha stragglers were unwilling to go any further and thus, they were left behind in Rangoon.

CHAPTER 4

ORDEAL AT MONYWA

The train journey had been quite uneventful, though the ticket Inspector came into the compartment and checked their tickets. Looking out of the compartment's windows, they saw an increasing number of Japanese troops and military vehicles, as the train chugged to the north. The train reached Mandalay during the morning of 10 August. Pritam Singh was quite helpful as he could fluently converse in Burmese and he knew the area quite well. From Mandalay Railway Station, Pritam guided them to Mandalay Bus Stand. Here, Pritam bought bus tickets for Monywa, and they all boarded a crowded, local bus. In the bus there was an overpowering smell of a popular fruit named *Durian* that was being carried and eaten by some travelers. The bus drove into Monywa, as it was getting dark. From the deserted bus stand, Pritam Singh guided them along darkened streets to the local Gurudwara.

There were a number of people living in the Gurudwara and many more frequently came and went, greatly raising the escapees' suspicions. Pritam Singh knew the Gurudwara's Granthi, a thin Sikh with *handlebar* moustaches, named Natha Singh. Pritam introduced them to Natha Singh as shop owners and friends from India. Natha explained that many people had been stranded in Monywa because of heavy fighting, that was taking place along the border with India. He also told them there was a Bengali Ayurvedic Doctor staying at the Gurudwara, nicknamed, "Babuji – Babuji". So, if anyone of them was unwell, he could easily be medically treated. A shop-keeper who kept shop near the Gurudwara, told Parab to be careful as there were many suspicious people in Monywa, who were either British or Japanese spies.

Ordeal At Monywa

They had planned to go on to Kalewa and from there to enter India. However, at Monywa, they were told it was impossible to travel through Kalewa, unless they held specific passes that had been issued by Japanese authorities. They, therefore, ventured to the office in town and applied to Japanese authorities for passes to proceed to Mawlaik and onwards to Kalewa. They met the Japanese Intelligence Officer (Lt Nomi) to get necessary passes to proceed to Mawlaik. Nomi spoke good English and asked them what they did for a living! They represented themselves as businessmen who owned two shops in Pegu. They said their parents had left for India in March, but the three of them had been held up at Mawlaik. They were concerned about their parents' welfare and wanted to bring them back from Mawlaik. Lt Nomi asked them to come back again after two days.

After the required waiting time was over, they went back and found their case had been shuttling between the offices of Japanese and Burmese authorities, ever since it had been submitted. They were told the matter had been forwarded to Burmese authorities (*Jiiikhai*), who had returned it to the Japanese. In extreme desperation, Balbir told Lt Nomi they were worried about their parents and would be grateful for written instructions on how to proceed in the matter. On the next day they discovered the case had been re-submitted to *Jijikhai*. They were told by Pritam, they could depend on an individual named Pillai, who would assist them. Pillai was a former PWD overseer, who lived adjacent to the Gurudwara. They met Pillai and told him about their predicament. Pillai listened to them carefully and said he would try to help them to get the required 'travel passes'.

As he had promised, Pillai operated quickly and obtained the necessary permission from *Jijikhai*, for the escapees to proceed to Mawlaik. But they still had to personally obtain the final approval from Japanese authorities. So Pillai accompanied them to Lt Nomi. However, the Japanese officer was quite annoyed to see them once again. He rudely turned them out of his office, but asked them to see him after an hour. In the meanwhile, Lt Nomi must have gone over their case for when they met him again he immediately announced he could grant them only two passes to proceed to Mawlaik. The third person would have to stay on at Monywa and report to

Lt Nomi every day till the others returned. They realized the third escapee was going to be held as a 'hostage' till their return to Monywa.

It was a ridiculous proposition from the Japanese officer and did not suit their future plans, as they had no intentions of returning to Monywa. What would happen to the 'hostage' who was to be left with Lt Noni? They could scarcely believe what they had been told! So, Balbir asked Lt Nomi for permission for the three of them to leave the office and discuss the matter in private. In an extremely disinterested manner, Nomi had waved them away. He did not look up, and began to peruse another file. They trooped out of the office and analyzed the shocking bit of information Lt Nomi had just given them. Disgusted with the attitude of authorities, they agreed there was no use of meeting Lt Nomi ever again. So, they set off for the Gurudwara, without saying a word, thereby leaving Pillai quite nonplussed.

At the Gurudwara they met Pritam Singh, who told them he had come to meet the Granthi. In disgust, they told Pritam about the suggestion made by Lt Nomi. Pritam heard them out patiently and surmised they should not shelve their travel plans, as they had not been officially debarred from traveling to Mawlaik. He said, he knew of an Indian trader named Thakur Singh who would surely help them travel to Mawlaik, as he knew some Japanese officers in Monywa. He promised to take them to Thakur Singh's house, on the next day.

Early next morning, Pritam Singh reached the Gurudwara and escorted took them to Thakur Singh's house. They walked through some very narrow streets, to reach Thakur Singh's abode. Here they were warmly welcomed by Thakur Singh, who asked them to be seated and prepared hot tea to drink. Pritam introduced them as ex POW, who had escaped from Japanese custody, at Singapore. They noticed Thakur Singh raise is eyebrows in surprise, when he learnt they were Indian Army officers who had escaped from a POW Camp in Singapore. Pritam Singh then said he had some urgent work to attend to, and left after consuming the tea. Thakur Singh sat with the escapees and discussed their proposed move to Mawlaik and Kalewa. He showed a great deal of interest in their plans to reach India. However, they had no reason to suspect his motives and settled down to enjoy his hospitality. Suddenly, he rose to his feet and told them he knew some Japanese officers who would surely grant them the required permission to travel to Mawlaik and Kalewa. He added that since the Japanese officers were planning to visit Rangoon, he would go and meet them before they left Monywa. He asked them to relax in the house while he went out to meet the Japanese officers. Not suspecting Thakur Singh's motives, the escapees were immensely pleased with their good luck. They settled down on the comfortable chairs to rest. Almost instantly, they fell asleep and never knew how quickly time flew. After about an hour or so, Thakur Singh was back with Japanese soldiers of *Kemptai* or Secret Japanese Military Police. The soldiers kicked their chairs and roughly roused the officers from their peaceful slumber. They were immediately arrested, before they could get up and try to make a get-away. While they were being led away, they realized that a terrible betrayal had been engineered by the Indian trader. They felt sickened and cursed themselves for trusting Thakur Singh with their plans. Thakur Singh talked with the Japanese soldiers on friendly terms, and apparently he knew them well. He consciously avoided the escapee's gaze, and slipped out of the house when they were being man-handled. Their wrists were bound by the Japanese soldiers and they were rudely kicked, shoved and dragged to Monywa Police Station.

On arrival at the Police Station, their wrists were untied and they were made to sit on the stone, verandah floor, with their possessions. A single Japanese soldier was left to guard them, while the others went inside the Police Station, happy with themselves for making a good catch! Not wasting a minute, Parab rose to his feet and asked the guard for permission to use the nearby latrine. In the latrine, he destroyed the precious map and other incriminating documents that were in his possession. Meanwhile, Balbir told the disinterested guard they were very tired and requested to to be allowed to brew some tea. There was a small open fire-place or '*chulah*', at the end of the verandah that they wanted to use. On the pretext of taking out tea leaves from his bundle, Balbir removed his incriminating documents, including the precious diary he had been writing ever since they had escaped from the POW Camp in Singapore. He kept a watch over his shoulder to see he was not being watched and burnt all the documents in the small fire he had lit. He also brewed some tea, and gave the guard a steaming, hot cup of the liquid. The other guards soon returned and conducted a detailed, body search. Their bundles were also searched, but nothing objectionable was found. However, the guards found the letter written in Hindi that had been given them by Prem Chand, in Mergui, to Parab. The escapees had promised to post the letter in India. They also found a rough, hand-drawn, sketch map of Akyab[1]* and a small account book in Gurmukhi. Fortunately, the guards could read neither Hindi nor Gurmukhi, so they merely dismissed the incriminating letter and Accounts Notebook, as documents of little consequence. Luckily, the sketch map did not have any suspicious notations by them, so they could easily feign ignorance and treat the sketch as just a piece of paper they had used for wrapping the note book that held details of their accounts, and had other notations in Gurmukhi and Hindi. Thus, the sketch map was discarded by the dis-interested guards as a piece of trash! At the end of the search, the guards were quite puzzled, as quite contrary to Thakur Singh's serious allegations, they had not found any incriminating documents or maps, to prove the arrested trio was Indian Army officers, who had escaped from a POW Camp in Singapore, and were proceeding to India.

The prisoners were interrogated and seriously threatened with death by be-heading, if they were found to be lying. From the questions asked during interrogation the easily surmised the Japanese were looking for under-cover Allied agents and informers, who they believed had been infiltrated into Burma through the active front-lines of Manipur. Surprisingly, they did not seem too interested in looking for escaped prisoners, and especially prisoners who had reportedly escaped from far-off Singapore and may be heading towards India! During their interrogation, the three officers did not deviate from the story they had perfected. The trio behaved as dumb refugees and insisted they were innocent civilians, who owned shops in Pegu. They said, they had been parted from their parents during the fighting in Burma. Their parents had proceeded towards India, and were last known to have been in Mawlaik / Kalewa. Thus, they were now looking for their parents. The *Kemptai* did not want to waste

---

1 While in Rangoon, Balbir had copied portion of a map of Burma that was hanging on a wall in Chartered Bank.

their time on dim-witted and scruffy looking civilians, who appeared to be genuine refugees, despite the Indian trader's vehement protestations.

Thus, the escapees were thrilled to see Thakur Singh being punched around his ears, by the annoyed Japanese interrogating officer and guards. Their joy knew no bounds, when they saw the rotten Thakur Singh being rudely thrown out from the Police Station, with well directed kicks in his pants! After their initial interrogations, they had been placed in cramped, 'solitary confinement' cells, located behind the Police Station. Once they were in the 'solitary confinement' cells, they softly called out to each other and were glad they could communicate. However, their new found joy was short lived as a Japanese armed guard stood outside the cells and angrily conveyed to them in 'sign language' they were not permitted to talk amongst themselves. He put a finger on his lips and tapped his rifle to threaten them with dire consequences, if they dared to speak in the cells. The prisoners sat on the cement floor and silently surveyed their little 'solitary confinement cells'. In horror, they discovered deep finger-nail scratches on the cell's cement plastered walls. The jagged, nail marks bore witness to innumerable torture sessions that must have taken place in the solitary confinement chambers!

The deep lines on the walls had greatly frightened the escapees. However, their long interrogation sessions, beatings and torture left them with little time and energy by the end of the day, to contemplate on the fate of these earlier prisoners. The interrogations continued, but the trio kept repeating their well rehearsed story. Although, the Japanese accepted the concocted story, they were not satisfied about two distinct issues. Firstly, they repeatedly asked for the location of their shops in Pegu, and secondly, they could not understand why the trio could not speak Burmese, despite their having supposedly lived in Burma were from families that owned two shops! In their desperation, the escapees had decided on fictitious locations of the shops in Pegu, and had passed on the location to one another, by loud whispers through the cell's windows. The 'whispered messages' were passed during early hours of the day, when they were sure the Japanese guards were fast asleep. They hoped the Japanese would not cross check their facts, as their knowledge about Pegu, was rather limited, and they knew they would be easily caught out.. About not knowing Burmese language, they had told their interrogators they had been sent for a good *public school* education to Singapore, at a young age. They had lived in 'boarding school' and were given an 'English medium' education. The Japanese officer had remained suspicious about their lack of knowledge of Burmese language, but their fluency in written and spoken English, gave great credence to their claims of having had a *public school* education, in Singapore. They were asked numerous details of Singapore, which they happily provided to their interrogators.

On 14 September, quite unusually all three prisoners were summoned together to office of Officer-in-Charge (OIC) of the Police Station. They were surprised to see Lt Nomi lolling in a chair, next to OIC of the Police Station. Lt Nomi seemed to know about their arrest and many details of their interrogation. Noni smiled and said they would be put on a train, the next day to return to Pegu. He added they would be given the necessary documents for their travel. He had insisted they were not to return to Monywa! Their relief was unimaginable at being told they were to be released. After being locked-up and tortured in Kempetai chambers for nearly a fortnight, the three officers found it hard to believe they were going to be released, unharmed from Japanese custody!

The Group Splits

On the next day (15 September), the three escapees bowed low and smiled humbly while bidding farewell to unsuspecting Japanese guards, who had herded them to Monywa Railway Station. At the Railway Station, they were given permits that allowed them to travel back to Pegu. When the train to Pegu arrived, the Japanese guards unceremoniously pushed them into a compartment. The guards remained on the Railway Platform till the train whistled twice and chugged out of Monywa. The escapees jumped off the train at the first stop after Monywa, and sat in the fields beyond the rail tracks. Here, they worked out their future plans.

They had learnt of large-scale Japanese troop movements towards India and it appeared some major enemy operations were taking place. After the nasty experiences in Japanese custody, they did not want to be caught up in the fighting. If caught, they were likely to be recognized and summarily executed. Thus, they decided to alter their future plans. Balbir and Parab wanted to give Monywa a wide berth and avoid Japanese build-up at the front-lines. They had also heard of American and Chinese forces operating in the north. Thus, they wanted to proceed north to Myitkyina and beyond, to contact the Allied forces.

However, Pritam did not agree with their views and felt that proceeding north would be far too dangerous, due to heavy fighting between Japanese forces with Chindits, and American & Chinese forces and also the difficult terrain in north Burma. After the unpleasant experience of incarceration, interrogations and torture at Monywa, they realized the difficulties involved in putting together a credible story for the Japanese interrogators to believe them. They knew the .next time around they may not be so lucky! They also realized it was impractical for a group of three members to successfully continue with the journey, without being arrested at some stage. Thus, the group mutually agreed to split into two parts. It was a sad parting and Pritam Singh decided to proceed to India, by himself, while Balbir and Parab proceeded north to Myitkyina.

Pritam had heard of a Sikh community and Gurudwara, at Chhangu (about 15 miles from Monywa). Thus, on 15 September when they got off the train to Pegu, Pritam left the other two officers and proceeded to the west[2]. However, as a contingency plan it was arranged for Balbir and Parab to retrace their steps and rejoin Pritam, if the northern route was found unsuitable for a further journey to India.

---

2 After parting ways with Balbir and Parab, Pritam proceeded to Chhangu, as planned. Here, he came in contact with an IA officer named Maj Mahabir Singh Dhillon (ex 5 Sikh), who had joined INA. Dhillon was being sent to India to recruit 'fifth column' agents for INA. Pritam went along with Dhillon through Kindat and Tamu, where they contacted one Capt MacDonald of Rajputana Rifles, on telephone. MacDonald arranged for them to pass through IA defensive positions. They reached 29 Infantry Brigade HQ, on 25 October 1942 and proceeded to India. Once in India, Pritam and Dhillon surrendered to the British authorities. During his detailed interrogation, he gave details of the 'escape' and told his interrogators about Balbir & Parab, and their plans to travel north to Myitkyina and contact Allied forces, in that area.

Indian refugees leaving Burma in large numbers - 1942

ROUTE FROM SINGAPORE TO INDIA

[MONYWA - SUMPRABAUM SECTION]

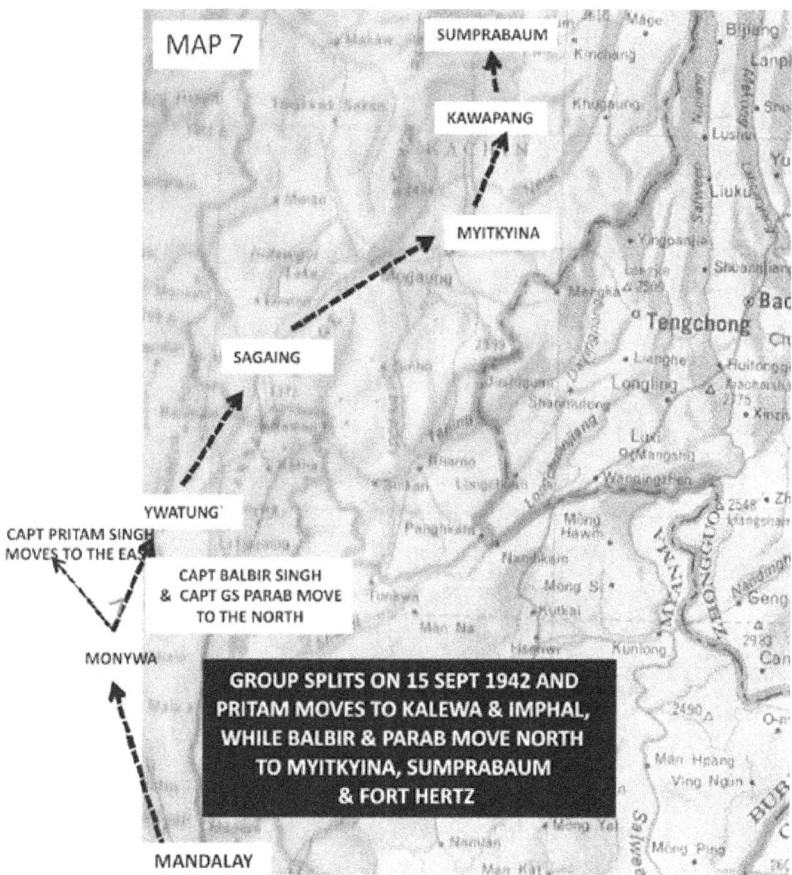

Chapter 5

TO INDIA AT LAST

After parting company with Pritam, Balbir and Parab proceeded to Ywatung by train, and arrived there on 16 September. At Ywatung they were put up in the house of a Railway Guard of Indian origin. Name of this Railway Guard had been furnished by Pillai, while they were in Monywa. The Railway Guard was a hospitable man and they spent a comfortable night at his house, located near the Ywatung Railway Station.

On the next day (17 September), they had difficulty in obtaining railway tickets for Myitkyina, as few trains were running to the north, because of the heavy fighting that was in progress in the area, between the Japanese and American-Chinese forces. They could see a great deal of military movement taking place by rail and on the roads. Waves of Japanese aircraft were also seen droning to the north. In the prevailing scenario, civilians were generally discouraged from traveling to the north. However, after waiting in long lines for a couple of hours, they were able to get tickets for onward travel to Sagaing. When they went to board the train, they found it carried Japanese troops in carriages, while military stores were loaded in closed trucks. Civilian passengers were unceremoniously packed in the open trucks. They climbed into an open truck and sat on hard, metal floor-boards. Fortunately, they were protected from heat of a burning sun, as there were dense clouds in the sky. It was a short journey and the train pulled into Sagaing, after they had travelled for a few uneventful hours.

Outside the Railway Station at Sagaing, was a bustling market-place. Balbir and Parab got off the open rail wagon and walked through the market stalls. On Parab'sn bright idea, they used some of their dwindling cash reserves to buy a large amount of washing soap. The soap was meant as evidence of their being petty traders, if they were questioned by the Japanese authorities. They planned to sell the soap in Myitkyina and possibly even earn some cash, for their further ventures! On returning to the Railway Station, they were pleased to find the train was still where they had left it, an hour earlier. They walked down the platform and climbed into the open wagon they had earlier occupied. They happily sat on the floor, without purchasing tickets for the journey from Sagaing to Myitkyina. Soon the train puffed out of the Sagaing Railway Station and made its way north, slowly through thick jungles and low hills. At every stoppage, they ducked down to the floor-boards, as they did not have tickets and were scared they may be arrested. However, their fears were unfounded and the train finally reached Myitkyina, as it was getting dark.

At Myitkyina, they stayed for two days in the house of an individual named Mohan Singh, who was a relative of Tara Singh. They had to ask directions from many people, before they could find Mohan Singh's house. Here, they met another Indian named Bahadur Singh, who was President of the newly formed Myitkyina Branch of IIL. They confided in Bahadur Singh, that they had been prisoners in Singapore. He was a shocking picture of 'open mouthed wonder', when they told him about their escape and added they were headed to India. They clearly remembered the great betrayal at the hands of Thakur Singh at Monywa, and so they told Bahadur Singh a slightly modified version of the story meant for Japanese authorities. Bahadur Singh gave them sound advice for their further move to India, and added they would need permits to enter the *'Putao Area'*. He even took them to the Japanese HQ, to get the necessary permits. At the HQ, they met an amicable Japanese officer, who spoke a bit of English. Thanks to the frequent interjections by Bahadur Singh, the Japanese were convinced about their refugee status and they received the necessary permits to travel to *'Putao Area'*. After talking to various people at Myitkyina they learnt that Japanese were seriously questioning civilians proceeding to the north, in any mode of mechanical transport. Therefore, they decided it was safer to travel the remaining 125 miles, to Fort Hertz, on foot. They knew it was going to be a difficult trudge to Fort

Hertz, in their ragged physical condition, but they were prepared to face any hardships on the way, but they did not want to repeat the awful time in Japanese detention, at Monywa.

On 23 September, they thanked Bahadur Singh and set out on foot for Sumprabaum. They frequently heard the deep, rumble of artillery fire, which assured them they were heading in the right direction and nearing the front-lines. They had to move cautiously, evade Japanese outposts and avoid their alert patrols. After the dismal days spent in POW Camps, the rigors of escape and their harrowing journey from Singapore, it was a wonderful feeling to finally be close to friendly Allied forces. Thus, with renewed energy, they walked along the sides of a deserted road to Kawapang. The road surface was uneven and it had deep pot-holes. The road had not been re-surfaced or tarred, after the previous year's monsoon rains. There were thick trees on both sides of the road and they came upon a few jungle clearings with villages and fields. Village dogs barked occasionally when they saw the two escapees, but they did not attempt to leave the shelter of the jungle clearings and get close to the escapees. Villagers had been informed by Japanese, that Chinese forces were advancing from the north. They had also been told to remain wary of Chinese brutality. They showed the villagers photographs of destroyed villages, reportedly in north Burma and recounted the looting and burning of villages. Therefore, it seemed very strange to Malay villagers, that while Japanese forces and civilians were moving back from Sumprabaum, these two strangers were walking towards the front lines in the north! Therefore, Malay peasants would stare in wonder and utter amazement at the two crazy strangers, who limped northwards! Occasionally, a Japanese military truck would roar past them, moving back with speed towards Myitkyina. Once they even saw a convoy of about 10-15 military trucks, moving back over the rutted road, with great speed. Whenever, they heard an approaching vehicle, both the officers would dash into the jungle and hide behind bushes or thick trees.

The weather had remained cloudy with intermittent showers, ever since they left Myitkyina. Puddles of water collected in the low lying ground whenever it rained. Thus, it was difficult to find a dry spot to sleep at night. But undeterred, both officers would curl up in the undergrowth and sleep fitfully, as they were exhausted by their exertions of the day's march. The incessant rains frequently soaked them and they had to walk and even sleep, in wet clothes. They would pass the night, huddled together for warmth and protection against more rain showers. It was truly a miracle that they did not fall ill. They were carrying roasted gram for their sustenance, and they often munched the gram while walking or when they sat down to rest. They were also carrying two packets of precious biscuits, which had been bought in a shop in Myitkyina. A single biscuit would be shared by both officers at the end of each day's march. The biscuit marked the end of each tough day, with a lot of pleasure. Eating of the biscuit was a great event for the escapees, and they would look forward to it for the entire day! They eagerly looked forward to munching on the delicious half-biscuit, in the evening. Just the thought of the biscuit, often got them through the miseries of each day. The precious, biscuit packets had been wrapped tightly in water-proof paper to save them from the frequent showers of rain. Their drinking water was carried in two glass bottles, which had once contained orange squash. They had found the bottles in a rubbish heap in Monywa, and stashed them away in their ragged bundles. Mouthfuls of roasted gram followed by deep gulps of water from the glass bottles formed a welcome meal for the two escapees!

Their torn and tattered canvas shoes had been wrapped with shoe-laces and bandages, to hold the worn soles together with the uppers. Walking, even slowly, had become sheer torture, as their feet were very painful due to deep cuts, foot-rot and large open blisters. Walking in wet shoes through the rain puddles, would badly hurt their swollen feet. To add to their misery, persistent dysentery was draining their strength, and they had neither money nor medicines to cure the recurring affliction. On 28 September, they walked into Kawapang. It was a small town with a market-place, shanty-town and some old, colonial bungalows on the jungle's edge. They spoke to many people in the bustling market-place, but could not find a place to spend the night. So, they went to one of the old and apparently deserted colonial bungalows at the edge of the jungle. They were about to enter the bungalow, when a Japanese soldier appeared from inside. On seeing the Japanese soldier, they swung around and began to run away from the bungalow. The soldier quickly recovered his composure and yelled at them to halt. They stopped in their tracks and instinctively raised their hands, without turning back. The soldier told them to follow him and he herded them to some Army tents that had been, pitched behind the bungalow. Here, a Japanese officer sat on a camp chair, reading an old Japanese news paper. They bowed low and told him their well rehearsed story. Balbir also showed him their passes, to reinforce the story. Luckily, he understood a bit of English and heard them out patiently and asked a few routine questions. When he was satisfied with their answers, he surprised them by asking what he could do to help them. They told him, they wanted to spend the night and move on in the morning. He nodded and told the soldier to take them to a dilapidated out-house adjacent to the tents, and allow them to spend the night.

The soldier took them to an out-house, where a detachment of about 10 – 20 Japanese troops was camping in the open. A large fire was burning brightly and there were enticing aromas in the air as the evening meal was cooked. There was also considerable activity taking around them, and some soldiers sat near the fire in various forms of undress. They could be heard talking and laughing loudly, as they dried their clothes and boots. They stopped near the fire and pointed to nearby rooms where they had been told to stay for the night. The Japanese troops around the camp-fire waved escort them on their way. The escort seemed to be more amicable after the officer had approved of their night's stay in the out-house of the bungalow.

There was large scale enemy activity all through the night, as convoys of military vehicles kept moving down the road towards Myitkyina. Headlights of these vehicles were not doused or dimmed, and it appeared the Japanese were withdrawing from the battle zone, in a great hurry and under severe Allied pressure. Meanwhile, protected from rain the escapees had a good sleep and they awoke feeling well rested and much better, than they had felt in a long while. Dawn had broken and there was broad daylight everywhere. However, outside their room they perceived a strange silence, so they went outside and cautiously looked around the place. They were pleasantly surprised to find that they were all by themselves at the bungalow, as the Japanese detachment had departed during the night.

Taking advantage of the favourable situation, they ducked into the jungle and began to walk rapidly. All the while, they kept parallel to the road. As the escapees were trudging forward painfully, they began to hear the deep crumps of mortar fire. Just then, two Japanese fighter aircraft thundered overhead. They were flying low and heading towards Sumprabum. Instinctively, the escapees took cover behind some thick trees. Once the aircraft had passed, they quickly rose to their feet and continued walking parallel to the road. All day long there was the roar of many more Japanese military vehicles speeding towards Myitkyina. Before it got dark, they halted and improvised a hideout, deep within a large expanse of dense undergrowth. Luckily, it did not rain during the night, although the two escapees had readied their hide-out for a downpour. Next morning, they were up early and commenced their dreaded walk, well before sunrise. Their feet were swollen and deep infection was causing them a raging fever. At times, they became delirious and mumbled incoherently among themselves. Whenever their minds were clear, they boosted each other's spirits with humorous, small talk. Deep inside, they both knew that friendly troops had to be contacted soon or with their rapidly deteriorating health, all would be lost. With each passing day they managed to move forward by virtue of sheer will-power and prayed for their terrible ordeal to end quickly.

During the next afternoon, they had just rounded a bend when they came face to face with Japanese soldiers of a large enemy group. Both sides were surprised by this chance encounter. However, before they could flee into the jungle, the leading Japanese soldiers quickly raised their rifles. The two escapees lifted their arms and they were captured. The Japanese were quite surprised to come across these two scruffy looking civilians, who were moving towards the front lines. The Japanese quickly bound the captive's wrists with small pieces of thin rope. The escapees were disgusted at the sudden change in their fortunes. The two officers looked around themselves and assessed they had been captured by an enemy company, of about 90 or 100 men. The company was commanded by an officer and seemed to be withdrawing under Allied pressure. They took the two captives back the way they had come. It was agonizing to return along the route they had so painstakingly traversed, not so long ago.

The Japanese halted for the night in a jungle clearing and fed the prisoners with their dry rations and gave them a drink of water. They were taken before the Japanese officer, who was sitting on a rock and rolling down 'puttees', from his olive-green breeches. He looked up as the two 'civilians' were brought before him. The officer ran a hand through his thinning hair that was damp with perspiration. He looked tired after the march and asked them in good English, as to who they were and where were they going?' Parab confidently gave out their well rehearsed story, while Balbir nodded and broke in now and again to reinforce a particular point. By now, they had become experts at reciting the concocted tale, with all appropriate emotions and expressions. Unfortunately, the officer appeared to be suspicious of their story, and he was not very impressed by their acting skills. They were alarmed, when he asked the sentry to call for the wireless set, as they thought he would check out their story and they would be caugiht out. When the wireless set arrived, he spoke to someone at the other end, rapidly in Japanese. After speaking on the wireless set for a while, he told the two officers they were to remain with his troops, who had halted for the night. Next morning, they were to accompany the column to Myitkyina. A sentry was posted to watch over them, as they lay on tall grass that they had folded down to form an improvised mattress. Both prisoners carefully watched the enemy for any signs of slackness. But, they found escape was not possible that night, as Japanese sentries remained on high alert against marauding Allied patrols.

As they lay on the grass, the two officers spoke softly to one another in Hindustani. They agreed that it was imperative they escaped on the next morning, otherwise the Japanese company would take them to a proper camp with hardened cells. Escape would be impossible from within a well guarded enemy camp. Parab reminded Balbir of how he had easily escaped from enemy clutches, after Battle of Slim River. He said it was not difficult and they could easily escape on the next day, when the column was moving through the jungle. Early next morning the Japanese moved out in two parties. Balbir and Parab were herded with the second party, which was commanded by a Japanese NCO. While walking with the Japanese patrol in the early morning mist, they exchanged glances and suddenly gave the Japanese a slip. As they crashed noisily through thick undergrowth, at any moment they expected to be hit by bullets in their backs. Excited shouts rang out from the enemy soldiers. They were lucky the Japanese fired only a few desultory shots and did not seriously pursue them into the jungle. It seemed the Japanese were happy to be withdrawing from the active frontline, and did not want to be delayed by the refugees. They seemed glad to be rid of the encumbrance of two unwanted prisoners!

Balbir and Parab bore the pain in their feet and moved with speed through the jungle. They carried their small bundles across their shoulders, as they ran through the thick jungle. Their chests burned as they noisily, panted for breath. As they were determined, not to be caught at the very end of their torturous journey, they kept running in the jungle, despite the intense pain in their feet. Remembering their days as cadets in Indian Military Academy, Dehradun, they tried to create a rhythm between their flailing feet and desperate gasps of breath. Although their weak bodies cried for the exertions to cease, they did not dare to stop and rest. They were free and they wanted to remain free, thus, they kept running hard in the jungle. They evaded a Japanese forward position. Enemy troops who manned the position were edgy and resorted to nervous shouts and random firing, but they never came out of their defensive position. Knowledge that there were enemy posts in the jungle, kept them moving fast, despite their pathetic physical state. Their great determination to be free can be gauged from the fact that they covered about 22 miles in five hours of nearly non-stop running in the jungle!

A little later, they saw a tired looking Japanese patrol approach from the direction of the front-line. They immediately stopped and tried to merge with the undergrowth, besides the track. But, they were not quick enough to hide. With his chest heaving desperately to take in air, Parab stood with his face to the jungle, pretending to be urinating. As the patrol drew abreast, Balbir bowed low and loudly said *'Konichiva'*. It was a greeting that had been beaten into their heads by the Japanese guards at Nee Soon POW Camp in Singapore. A Japanese NCO returned the greeting, but the soldiers kept moving on and did not bother to stop and question the two unkempt civilians! It seemed the Japanese were in a great hurry to get away from the active front-lines, and the menacing rumble of artillery and mortar fire seemed to have increased considerably. Then sound indicated that the battle-lines were getting closer.

Around mid-day on 5 October, the two officers had just passed Milestone 105, when the stillness of the jungle was broken by deep thuds of a Bren gun firing. Bullets cracked viciously overhead as the two escapees dived for cover and hid behind some boulders. They were certain the fire had come from friendly forces, as they distinctly recognized the deep thudding sound of the 'friendly' Bren Gun firing at them. Though, their happiness knew no bounds, they realized the friendly force had to be contacted fast, before the Bren Gun fire turned accurate and gunned them down. They made desperate calls, both in Hindustani and English to be heard by the Allied patrol at the other end. With lingering doubts about the two individuals who were shouting in Hindustani and English, the Allied troops finally decided to investigate the ragged fugitives, instead of shooting them dead!

Cautiously, a few soldiers dressed in olive-green (OG) uniforms, stepped out of their concealed positions. They covered one another and advanced carefully towards the fugitives. They had their .303 Lee Enfield rifles and Sten guns placed against their hips and were ready to shoot, as they began to walk across the intervening ground. As they drew closer, Parab waved his bare hands from behind the boulders. Cautiously, the soldiers approached the boulders. Once they saw the fugitives were unarmed, they put their weapons down, and relaxed. The senior NCO with the patrol asked who they were and what they were doing in the jungle. They were amazed to learn the two ragged individuals were IA officers, who had escaped from a Japanese POW Camp in far-way Singapore! With a warm smile, the senior NCO told Balbir and Parab, they were a patrol of Kachin Scouts on a mission to ambush Japanese stragglers. Along with ambush party, they moved back to the patrol base, which was located in the jungle and well away from the road. Here, they were given a cup of hot tea, from a Thermos Flask, while they waited for the remainder patrol to return. The other part of the patrol was moving on three elephants under a VCO, and it returned after about an hour. The senior NCO reported to the surprised VCO and introduced the two officers to him.

Ordeal At Monywa

After a brief halt, camp was struck and they were helped onto an elephant. It seemed unreal to be sitting comfortably, while the huge beast plodded forward, swaying rhythmically from side to side. Some members of the patrol sat on the other two elephants, while alert members led the way on foot, with weapons held ready to open fire. A few Kachin Scouts walked behind the lumbering beasts, and provided protection to the rear of the patrol. After a couple of hours of moving through the thick jungle, they entered the small town of Sumprabaum and made their way to the nearby Army camp.

The camp was located on a small hillock, about a mile out of town and protected with an earthen bund with bunkers, bamboo fence and a carpet of sharpened bamboo stakes (panjis). The 'panjis' were embedded in the ground and formed a formidable obstacle. After the patrol and elephants had entered the camp, they halted at a small e play-ground within the camp, while the heavy wooden gates were slammed shut. The two officers were helped to the ground by smiling Kachin soldiers, while others held the taken to the Post Commander, named Maj Leach. The Post Commander wore khaki shorts below a crumpled OG bush-shirt. The bush-shirt appeared to have seen a lot of sun, as it had nearly lost its OG colour. The VCO had reported the safe return of patrol and added he had brought along two IA officers, who said they had escaped, most unbelievably from a POW Camp in faraway Singapore! Leach adjusted his Australian bush-hat over a head of short, light coloured hair, and stood up to receive the two ragged figures, who were limping towards him.

Smiling broadly, he shook hands with Balbir and Parab, and enthusiastically thumped them on the back. He sat down and waved the two officers to sit on two bamboo stools placed before him. After recording the officer's name, army number and unit, he asked them for details of their escape from enemy custody. They briefly recounted their adventures and Leach was totally dumbstruck by what he heard. He urgently rose to his feet and called for the field-telephone. When the phone was brought to him, he cranked it hard. He was soon connected, and spoke at length with his superior officer at Fort Hertz. He was told to send both the officers to Fort Hertz, where they would be put on board a USAF aircraft proceeding to Dinjan (India), on the next day. After replacing the handset he repeated to the two officers what he had just been told by his superior officer at Fort Hertz.

The officers were taken to the *'langar'* (Indian troops kitchen), for a sumptuous dinner of hot rice, lentils and pieces of deep fried, chicken. After dinner, they were escorted to a large thatched hut. In the hut, they were pleasantly surprised to find two wooden cots had been placed on the floor of hard, packed earth. Spread on the beds was real bedding, comprising a cotton mattress, clean, white bed-sheets and fluffed-up pillows, in a clean, white, pillow case. Within minutes both escapees were soundly asleep on the comfortable beds. The pleasure of lying on a real cot, in a secure environment and after the first full meal in six long months, did not allow them to remain awake for long!

On the next morning (6 October), they wore fresh, new uniforms, provided by the Camp's Clothing Store. They were pleasantly surprised to find field epaulettes bearing Capt's rank, had been affixed on their well ironed, cotton, OG uniform shirts. They were wearing Capt's field epaulettes after a very long time, and it felt very good, indeed. In addition to three cloth stars, the epaulettes were embroidered with *'Kachin Scouts'* at the ends. It was an honour to don epaulettes bearing the inscription of *'Kachin Scouts'*. They were also greatly pleased they did not have to conceal they were IA officers. They were taken to the MI Room, where Capt Chatterjee, IMS, MO with Kachin Scouts, washed and bandaged their badly, bruised feet and gave them potent medicines for their ailment of dysentery.

Since early hours of the morning, a deep rumble of artillery fire could be heard and a flight of fighter aircraft roared past at low altitude. The flight of fighter aircraft went over the trees, shaking everything in the room. They assumed a major operation was in progress in the neighboring area. Around midday, they heard the drone of a single transport aircraft and saw a lone DC-3 (Dakota) aircraft circle lazily overhead. It dipped down and landed on the nearby landing-strip. The field telephone jangled and Maj Leach spoke with someone at the landing strip. Putting down the receiver, he yelled to his runner to summon the jeep. *'The plane is here for you lads and you're off to Fort Hertz. Cheerio and good luck, you lucky fellows'*, he announced breezily. Soon an open jeep came around and stopped before the hut. The escapees hefted their bundles into the jeep and returned to thank Maj Leach. They shook hands with Leach, saluted and got into the jeep. The driver gunned the engine and the vehicle raced to the landing strip, its tires loudly crunching loudly on the loose gravel.

The sky was grey and covered with clouds. Two, USAF DC-3 (Dakota) aircraft stood on the landing strip. The jeep moved to the aircraft that had just landed. The aircraft stood at the centre of the air-strip, and it was positioned for take-off. The jeep stopped near the aircraft and the two officers got off and walked forward with their few belongings. The aircraft had its fuselage door open and a metal ladder was lowered to the ground. A USAF Sergeant (Sgt) in grey over-alls was sitting on the lowest step of the ladder and whistling absently. While he whistled, the Sgt was aimlessly throwing pebbles into tall grass beside the air-strip. As Balbir and Parab approached the stairway, the NCO rose to his feet and pointed upwards to the open door of the aircraft. He obviously knew they were to be taken to Fort Hertz. The officers mounted the metal stairs and ducked into the fuselage of the plane. The USAF Sgt followed them into the plane and banged the door shut. After adjusting the door-clamps, he gave a thumbs-up signal to the pilot, through the open cockpit door. The Sgt lowered himself onto a folding seat near the closed door, and again began to softly whistle his tune. The co-pilot entered the fuselage and shook hands with Balbir and Parab. He too wore grey over-alls and asked the officers to sign on a typewritten sheet of paper, clipped to a small board. He then said something to the NCO and ducked back into the cockpit [see Map 8].

The pilot and co-pilot could be seen from the fuselage, as they sat on their elevated seats and peered intently through of the windscreen. The aircraft engines fired repeatedly, and all of a sudden the left side propeller began to rotate, slowly. Gradually, the propeller's speed increased and the left side engine also revved up, with a loud roar. Then, the engine on the right side fired up, and the propeller began to rotate. Soon the propeller had picked up its speed and both propellers were rotating at high speeds, with a thunderous roar. Blasts of air from the propellers flattened the grass near the runway and shook some leaves off the nearby trees. The aircraft vibrated violently on the runway, as both engines attained full power. The pilot looked back at them briefly, nodded with a smile, flashed a 'thumbs up' sign and released the plane's brakes. The DC-3 lurched forward like a wild stallion, pushing the passengers back into their seats. It roared down the open airstrip and picked up more speed. About halfway down the runway, the aircraft gently rose from the ground and its wheels folded into their receptacles below the wings, with a jarring thud. The engine sound smoothened greatly, after the wheels had folded away. The flight was short, and soon the plane was circling the airfield at Fort Hertz. The landing was bumpy and left them shaken, but it had surely been better than walking on the ground! The NCO gave them a toothy grin and raised a thumb to indicate that they were on the ground. The pilot steered the plane towards a tin roofed building, which stood next to a low brick tower, the improvised control tower of the airstrip.

News of their arrival seemed to have spread like wild-fire, for they could see about a dozen people standing beside the runway, near the building. The plane came to a halt and the NCO opened the fuselage door and lowered the metal ladder. He beckoned towards the two officers to come to the door. Balbir and Parab went down the ladder and saluted a tall, thin Lt Col, who was there to receive them. He returned their salutes and introduced himself as Lt Col Murray. They shook hands and he motioned them towards the building. He asked them to leave their baggage in the aircraft itself. Meanwhile, the pilot had walked up to the open fuselage door. Lt Col Murray looked up and told him to have the aircraft re-fuelled, as they would shortly be taking off for Tinsukia, in India. The pilot nodded, saluted Murray and ducked back into the aircraft. Murray led the way to the building, followed by Balbir and Parab. Here, they were introduced to officers of the Fort Hertz garrison, who had come to the air-strip on hearing sensational news of their arrival from Singapore. They all went into the tin roofed building, which doubled as Control Tower and Officers Mess. The waiting officers complimented them and shook their hands with great pleasure. They were thumped on the backs and a tall officer said with a broad grin, '*Very well done, chaps. We're going to give it back to those bloody Japs!*'

Capt Balbir Singh and Capt GS Parab board a DC-3 (Dakota) aircraft at Sumprabaum, Burma, on 6 October 1942. Another DC-3 aircraft waits on the runway.

They entered a large room where numerous chairs had been placed in rows. A map of Burma, Thailand and Malaya had been tacked onto a large black-board and placed near a wooden lecture stand, before the rows of chairs. Soon, everyone had entered the room and taken their seats. Balbir and Parab had been asked to be seated in the front row of chairs. Lt Col Murray stood behind the improvised lecture stand and faced the audience. He cleared his throat loudly and formally welcomed Capt Balbir Singh and Capt GS Parab to Fort Hertz. Murray went on to briefly explain how the two officers had made the remarkable escape from a POW Camp in Singapore and worked their way to Fort Hertz in Burma. On hearing Murray, there was an audible gasp from the audience. With a thin wooden pointer, he indicated the route they had followed, on the map tacked to the board. He then requested one of the escapees to come forward and narrate their adventures. Capt Balbir Singh glanced at Parab, rose and went forward to the lecture stand, while Lt Col Murray returned to his seat. Balbir looked around the audience. To his surprise, he noticed the DC-3 pilot was sitting in a corner, quite distinctive in his grayish-blue, flying overalls.

Balbir began his narration by explaining the ravaged situation in Singapore, after the bastion had fallen to Japanese forces. He described the conditions in POW Camps in Singapore, followed by details of their escape. The audience listened to the exciting account of their travels through Malaya, Thailand and Burma, in rapt attention. There were many questions about their escape from the POW Camp, crossing the IB to Thailand, the jungle crossing to Burma, the torturous time at Monywa and their re-capture and escape on the jungle track beyond Kawapang. There was a short break, followed by a long 'questions and answers session'. There were many questions and the session took nearly an hour, as the audience wanted a lot of information of the incredible escape and their harrowing journey. When there were no more questions, Balbir thanked the audience and moved back to his seat.

Spontaneously, the audience rose to their feet and sounds of loud applause filled the room. Balbir and Parab were highly embarrassed and did not know whether to stand or to keep sitting. So, they stood up, nodded on either side to show their appreciation and thanked those who were standing near them. After a cup of tea in Officers' Mess, Balbir and Parab shook hands with most of the officers and walked back to the aircraft. The DC-3 aircraft had been refueled and stood ready on the runway. With long strides, the pilot overtook them, climbed the stairs and ducked into the open fuselage door. The NCO stood at the foot of the stairs with his usual grin. As they reached the ladder, Balbir and Parab turned and saluted smartly, before climbing into the aircraft. Some large bundles wrapped in khaki canvas had been loaded into the aircraft at Fort Hertz, and they were lashed at the centre of the fuselage. After taking-off, the aircraft took large circles, and climbed above the thick, puffy, clouds. It soon settled into a level and high altitude flight to India. The officers looked down through the oval windows and saw low hills and dense tree cover. There were dark clouds on the horizon, indicating air turbulence and a bumpy flight. The engines soon settled into a steady drone and once again the officers nodded off into a deep sleep.

They did not know when the pilot walked through the open door to the cockpit and came to their seats, leaving the co-pilot to handle the controls. They woke to find the pilot standing before them. He shouted above roar of the engines, '*Hi, I'm Dave. I was sure impressed to hear what you guys have done and the terrible times you have been through. I must say, you both are real heroes and I am delighted to fly you on the last leg of your journey to India! I shall be honoured to shake your hand, Sir.'* He smiled and thrust his open palm towards them. One by one they shook hands with the USAF pilot. He turned, had a word with the NCO near the door, and staggered back into the cockpit. Flying over the hilly jungles, seemed an unreal dream, after the torturous marches. One after another, both officers fell asleep again, and dozed fitfully as the aircraft droned over the Burmese jungles and headed towards India.

Before they knew it, the NCO was shaking them awake. *'Wakey, wakey Sirs'* he said with a smile, *'Put on your safety belts. We'll shortly be landing at Tinsukia in India'.* Balbir and Parab stretched their weary limbs and affixed the safety belts with loud clicks. They peered out of the oval windows and saw thick, white clouds towering around the plane. Occasionally, through gaps in clouds they could see low hills, about 2000 feet below the aircraft. The thick jungle canopy soon gave way to fields of ripening paddy and isolated villages with thatched huts that dotted the area. It was a feeling of great joy, to be flying over India, and they could not believe their good luck. The aircraft circled over a large township and gradually began to lose height. Suddenly, there was a loud thud that shook the aircraft. They knew the landing gear had been lowered. A road could be seen, with a few military vehicles moving on it. Brick houses with flat, cement roofs lined the road. The aircraft kept dropping lower and soon they could see people moving on the roads. The sound of the engines changed and a wire fence flashed past. The plane had descended to almost to ground level and it rushed over a stretch of deep, grey coloured skid-marks on the tarmac. These long, skid marks had been made by the tires of countless aircraft that had landed at Tinsukia.

With its tires squealing loudly, the DC-3 (Dakota) aircraft touched down at Tinsukia and came to a halt at the far end of the runway. The aircraft's propellers continued to turn at high speed, as the aircraft turned around and moved to one side of the runway. Here, it halted adjacent to a red brick building with a sloping roof of tin sheets. After the plane had come to a halt, the USAF Flight NCO again became active. He undid the clamps, opened the aircraft door and lowered the metal ladder to the ground. He then gestured to the two passengers, to follow him down the ladder. The officers rose from their seats, and walked to the entrance of the cockpit and thanked both the pilots. They walked back, picked up their ragged bundles and climbed down the metal ladder. The Sgt stood on the tarmac, with his hands on the steel ladder, as the officers came down to the tarmac. They were thrilled when their feet touched the tarmac. Instinctively, both officers bent over and touched the soil of India with their lowered hands.

A cool breeze was blowing, as their bandaged feet touched the ground. Balbir and Parab took a deep breath and looked around with their heads held high. They were finally on Indian soil. It was the moment they had eagerly waited for, during the long and miserable months of hardship and uncertainty. Surprisingly, everything appeared to be the same as before and there were no special feelings of triumph or success. But, they both felt great joy that their ordeal was over. Balbir and Parab looked at each other with a big smile on their faces that hid innumerable feelings and emotions! Looking back, the last few months appeared to have been part of a horrible dream. But, all that was behind them. All that mattered now was the fact they had finally made it back to India. They wanted to jump for joy and yell with joy loudly. They could hardly believe they were alive and free. Nothing else seemed to matter anymore. Their eyes were moist with emotions, and they embraced one another. Balbir said aloud, *'Ganga congratulations, we have finally reached India. Honestly, there were times I thought we'd never make it back'*. Parab looked at Balbir, smiled and nodded in agreement.

An IA Capt was waiting for them at edge of the runway. He was dressed in smart OG, 'walking-out' dress and wore a brown 'Sam Browne' crossed belt and shining, brown, leather Oxford Pattern (OP), shoes. He had on a field hat with a wide brim that was turned up to one side. On seeing the two officers walk out from the aircraft, he stepped forward, saluted and shook hands. Balbir and Parab felt quite ragged and slovenly dressed before the smart young officer, despite their fresh uniforms. He said, *'Welcome home, Sir! I am Capt Siddique, and I have orders to take you to Jorhat, where you are to meet Gen Wavell'*.

They knew the escape adventure had ended, but many new adventures lay ahead. A lot of formalities were to be completed, before they could recollect their thoughts of the tumultuous times they had experienced. They thought of the intensive operations they had fought down the Malayan Peninsula, and of their difficult days at the POW Camps. They re-collected details of their escape, and the difficult times on the way. They sadly thought of the colleagues who had been killed during the vicious battles and the many others who they had left behind in the torturous, POW Camps in Singapore. Pritam too, came into their thoughts and they hoped and prayed he too had safely reached India. They could hear the USAF NCO whistle the familiar tune once more, as they walked away from the aircraft with Capt Siddique. They moved towards the waiting jeep. The USAF NCO's whistled tune gradually became faint as they walked from the aircraft and neared the jeep.

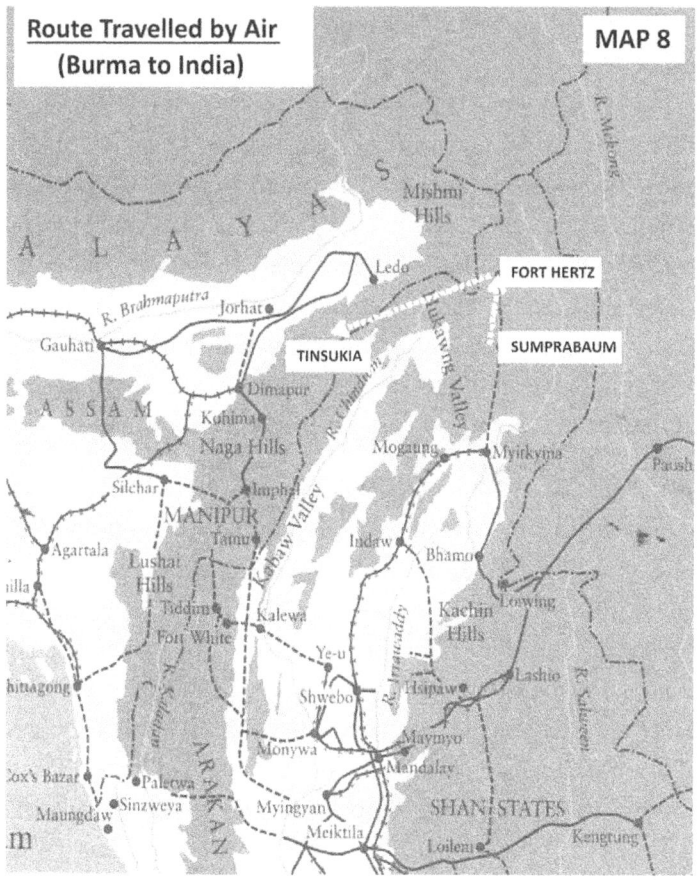

CONCLUSION

Racked with malaria, stomach ailments and grossly underweight, Capt Balbir Singh and Capt GS Parab reached India after nearly six months as fugitives in enemy territory. Their supreme determination and courage had helped them cover nearly 2000 miles across hostile jungles and through Japanese held territories. They were among the initial survivors to reach India after the fall of Singapore and give a detailed account of the locations of Japanese occupation forces in Malaya and Burma. Balbir had a raging fever, when they landed in India. From Tinsukia, they had been driven to Jorhat, where they met Gen AE Wavell, Overall Commander of Allied Forces in Burma, and it was a pleasant meeting. After they had given a detailed account of their journey, Wavell had shown great concern about their poor physical condition. He told his staff officers to send them to hospital in Calcutta (now Kolkata), for medical treatment.

On the next day, Balbir and Parab were driven to Manipur Road (now called Dimapur) Railway Station. Here they boarded a train to Calcutta. For the next couple of days, they had a chance to relax and sleep in the train to Calcutta, which was hauled by a steam locomotive. When they were not sleeping, the officers looked out of the window of the comfortable First Class compartment. Balbir was intrigued by a framed map of the area, affixed on the wood paneled wall, above a steel wash basin. He sighed when he remembered the decrepit trains in which they had traveled in Malaya, Thailand and Burma. How he wished they had such a wonderful map to consult during their travels. In their waking hours, the officers would look out of the windows and let their minds wander over the difficult times of their harrowing journey.

Conclusion

It was dark when the train pulled into the well lit and busy main platform of Calcutta Central Railway Station. Innumerable soldiers from various parts of the world could be seen moving about, wearing different patterns of service uniforms. They could make out soldiers from India, Africa, Britain, Australia and USA, moving on the platform. Amongst the soldiers, were tall and well built members of Military Police. These personnel moved in pairs and remained in step with one another. Two nursing orderlies received Balbir and Parab and guided them to an ambulance, parked in the corner of a large parking lot. There were three more ambulances in the parking lot. Serious battle casualties were off-loaded from the train on stretchers and loaded onto the ambulances.

At the large Military Hospital (MH), they were taken to the Officers' Ward. Eurasian nurses on duty, issued them with grey flannel night suits. They were examined by a team of doctors, fed a light dinner and given medicines for fever, malaria and dysentery. Antiseptic ointment was applied on their painful feet, which were then bandaged. They spent next 15 days at the hospital in Calcutta, where the fever, malaria and dysentery were treated. With a wholesome diet and rest, they quickly added some weight to their wasted frames. On their discharge from MH, they boarded a train to New Delhi. The journey took two days, and they were feeling much better, as the train neared the beautiful city of Delhi.

At Delhi Railway Station, a small detachment from a Gurkha Battalion, under a British officer, had come to receive them. They were taken to Red Fort. Here, they were billeted in a segregated portion of the historic fort. They were kept in a middle sized room that had two beds, a writing table and an attached toilet. They were told not to leave the room, without permission. Occasionally, when they looked out of the front door, they saw a couple of soldiers guarding their room. Balbir and Parab knew they were under a form of loose arrest that was called 'house arrest'. Daily, they were escorted to a side section of Red Fort, where detailed interrogations were conducted[1]. During these interrogations, they

---

1 During his interrogations in New Delhi, Balbir was pleasantly surprised to find a familiar face. The Chief Interrogator had been Professor of History at Government College, Lahore, when Balbir was a student at the College. Now, he was now an Emergency Commissioned Officer and had been assigned the task of interrogating the two officers. After daily interrogations, they would both find time to recount their old days at Lahore,

were asked to give a detailed explanation of their confinement, escape and journey to India. They had to make an estimate of the strength of enemy troops at different locations[2].

As the war situation with Japan was highly volatile in 1942, Balbir and Parab were suspected of being members of INA who had been infiltrated into India, by the Japanese. While talking to their interrogators, they were relieved to learn that Capt Pritam Singh had arrived safely in India. Details given by Pritam during his interrogation, helped convince the authorities they were not Japanese agents. Their incredible story kept the authorities spellbound.

It was finally accepted, Balbir and Parab were not Japanese agents. Once the authorities agreed the officers had indeed escaped from Singapore and undertaken the incredible journey to India, there was a marked change in the attitude of British authorities, for the better. One of the positive indicators was the removal of guards outside their room. They were now free to walk within Red Fort. During their walks, Balbir took Parab to the Officers' Mess, which was located directly above the main entrance of Red Fort, and in line with main-street of Chandni Chowk. Here, Parab was shown bullet holes in the walls, dating to the fighting during Sepoy Mutiny of 1857-58[3].

---

during the early 1930s !

2 The following locations and strength of Japanese military forces (May to August 1942) was assessed and given out to the interrogators:-

- Singapore   - 15, 000.
- Penang   - 5, 000.
- Alor Star   - 1, 200.
- Mergui   - 400.
- Tavoy   - 200.
- Moulmein   - 1, 500.
- Pegu   - 1, 500.
- Rangoon   - 10, 000.
- Monywa   - 2, 500.
- Myitkyina   - 1, 000 – 1, 200.

3 In 1936, after being commissioned from Indian Military Academy, Dehradun, Balbir did a year-long attachment with 2nd Battalion, Royal Fusiliers, in New Delhi. His company was posted in Red Fort and the officers would dine in Officers' Mess, located above the main-entrance to Red Fort.

Conclusion

After reaching New Delhi, they had been permitted to write letters to their families. On receiving the first letter, their families were astounded and most unbelieving. This was because they had been officially informed that all three officers had been captured in Malaya and shot dead by a Japanese firing squad. The false information had been cunningly spread by Japanese, to dissuade other personnel from escaping from POW Camps in Singapore. However, Military Intelligence authorities had received the false reports from operatives in Singapore, and accordingly the officers' families had been informed by Army HQ. Thus, receiving the first letter from the officers and news of their arrival in India was indeed a very joyous occasion.

For the daring escape from Singapore, and their nearly six month long journey through Malaya, Thailand and Burma, Capt Balbir Singh, Capt GS Parab and Capt Pritam Singh were awarded Military Cross. In February 1943, Balbir and Parab received their gallantry awards from Lord Linlithgow, the British Viceroy in India, during a glittering parade at the large square on Kingsway (now called Vijay Chowk on Rajpath). Later, all three officers received congratulatory letters from Field Marshal AE Wavell, Commander-in-Chief in India. Copy of the letter received by Capt Balbir Singh is at Appendix 'C'.

Military Cross

Appendix 'A'

EVASION BY CAPT GS PARAB AFTER BATTLE OF SLIM RIVER

Capt GS Parab was one of the survivors of the enemy onslaught on 4/19 Hyderabad Regt at Slim River during night of 6/7 January 1942. He had been separated from the Unit when Japanese tanks and infantry had broken through his company's defences. He made his way back after exciting adventures behind Japanese lines, over a period of the next several days. When the initial tank attacks took place, Parab was with his men in the trenches. As Japanese tanks raced through the Unit followed by waves of infantry, Parab found himself isolated in the jungle. In the darkness, he made his way south, through the jungle. Near Tanjong Malim he joined a party of officers and men, including Lt Col Deakin of 5/2nd Punjab. While moving towards Kuala Lumpur the group clashed with a strong Japanese column and they were dispersed.

Alone once more, Parab continued to the south. He was ably guided by the steel railway tracks that shone in the dark jungle. While walking through the jungle, he was suddenly seized by some Japanese soldiers and put to work on a damaged bridge. However, after carrying stones for about an hour or so, he managed to escape into the nearby jungle and reach Kuala Lumpur. The Japanese were already in occupation of the city and they were busy looting shops and homes. Parab hid himself behind a wall, in a narrow alley and watched the row of stores in front of him. Everything appeared peaceful and some elderly women could be seen walking in the street, carrying bags of groceries.

He was elated when he saw a Japanese soldier go into a store, leaving his bicycle unattended outside the shop. Without batting an eyelid, Parab sprinted from the alley and reached the store, where the bicycle had been propped against the wall. Without a backward glance, he confidently mounted the Japanese bicycle and rode off. As he rode down the street he felt wonderful to be mobile again after trudging endlessly through the thick jungle. Carefully avoiding Japanese held localities, Parab cycled furiously towards the 'front-line. After a while, he was fortunate to meet the Battalion withdrawing to the south after fighting the dreadful Battle of Slim River.

The Unit had halted during its withdrawal, and all ranks were resting on both sides of the jungle road. All of a sudden they saw a smiling, Capt Parab come riding down the road on a Japanese bicycle. When he went missing during the heavy fighting at Slim River, it was assumed he had been killed in battle, like so many others. The incongruous sight of Parab riding on a Japanese bicycle made the men smile and they began to cheer. After a long time, something nice had happened to make the troops laugh and cheer. The loud cheering caused many a head to turn in the depleted ranks of Argyll and Sutherland Highlanders, who were over-taking the Unit to lead the Brigade's withdrawal.

Appendix 'B'

GIST OF ADDRESSES MADE AT SINGAPORE, AFTER THE SURRENDER

Address by Maj Fujiwara, (speech was delivered in Japanese, translated in English, by Lt Konishita and into Hindustani by Col Niranjan Singh Gill).

'In ten weeks time, the mighty Japanese armed forces have conquered Malaya and the invincible fortress of Singapore. The British Empire is dwindling down. Japan is fighting to free the Asiatics from dominance of the Anglo-Saxon race, and to form Greater East Asia under the leadership of Dai Nipon. For this purpose Japan wants to drive the English from India and wants the co-operation of all Indians.

The Japanese have no designs on India, as General Tojo has already declared. It is a shame that 400 million people should be the slaves of 45 million people. If all the Indians co-operate sincerely in achieving the freedom of India, the English can be driven out easily without shedding blood.

You will see for yourself, for a short time you will be kept as prisoners of war, but you shall be treated far better than the Europeans. After some time, you will be free like the other Indian soldiers who were captured in the north.

I shall end by telling you that I look upon all Indians as my brothers'.

Address by Capt Mohan Singh (in Hindustani).

'In the first week of the campaign, I was separated in the jungle with a small party, including Capt Akram Khan. I was not captured as a prisoner of war, but several high Japanese officials approached me. After a few few days of talking with Japanese, Capt Akram Khan and I came to the conclusion that Great Britain was sure to lose the war and Axis powers were going to win. Therefore, it was a golden opportunity to join with the Japanese and obtain India's freedom. For this purpose the Japanese had promised to help us in every respect. After their assurances, I started the formation of Indian National Army, out of prisoners who had been captured on the mainland of Malaya.

The English have treated the Indians very badly, therefore, I appeal to all Indian prisoners-of-war to join this movement. In the campaign, Indian troops used to be on the front-lines, while English troops stayed in the rear. Whenever, Indian troops withdrew, English troops, who lived behind in comfort, shot them down. This had happened often, and especially in Singapore.

While you are in the POW camps you will be given lectures from time to time on India's glorious history. You will do normal training in the camps, but you will provide fatigue parties when the Japanese require them'.

Address by Giani Pritam Singh (in Hindustani).

'When I came to know Indian troops were in Malaya, I asked myself what were they fighting for? They were going to lose their lives for nothing. India is not the enemy of Japan; the English are the enemies of Japan and they want Indians to fight the Japanese! Therefore, I organized my party in Bangkok and followed the Japanese troops with intentions of saving Indian lives and helping the Japanese.

I will tell you how I achieved my object. My men used to go to the firing line and shout to Indian soldiers not to fight the Japanese, but to come over and join them. My men very often succeeded in their work and saved a lot of lives.

I sincerely hope that all Indians will join the great movement of Indian National Army (INA), started by Capt Mohan Singh'.

Appendix 'C'

LETTER FROM FIELD MARSHAL WAVELL TO CAPT BALBIR SINGH, MC. (4/19 HYDERABAD REGIMENT)

NEW DELHI.

31st March, 1943.

Dear Captain Balbir Singh

I offer you my very best congratulations on the award of the Military Cross in connection with your escape from enemy hands, and wish you all good luck in the future.

Yours sincerely

A.P. Wavell

Field Marshal,
Commander-in-Chief in India.

Captain BALBIR SINGH, M.C.,
4/19th Hyderabad Regiment.

Appendix 'D'

BRIEF HISTORY OF AZAD HIND FAUJ / INDIAN NATIONAL ARMY (INA)

The Azad Hind Fauj / Indian National Army (INA) was formed in 1942, from Indian prisoners of war (POW), captured by Japanese forces during the fighting in Malaya and Singapore. It was created to counter the British forces in Asia. Capt Mohan Singh became the INA's first leader[1]*, and Maj Iwaichi Fujiwara was the Japanese intelligence officer who worked out all the arrangements necessary to create the INA. Capt Mohan Singh had been captured during the fighting at Jitra (Malaya). As per plans, INA was to be trained to fight the British and other Allied forces in South-East Asia. The Japanese had sent intelligence agents to South-East Asian countries from the late 1930s onward, and they had established contact with the considerable population of South Asians, who were residents in Malaya, Singapore, Thailand, Burma, and other parts of the region. The Japanese aim was to use and benefit from the nationalism of Asian peoples in constructing what they called their "Greater East Asia Co-Prosperity Sphere." With their opening victories in the war, from December 1941 through the early months of 1942, the Japanese captured large numbers of Indian prisoners, particularly during their victory at Singapore, in February 1942. Some 40,000 to 50,000 IA soldiers were recruited for a training corps of South Asian residents in Southeast Asia.

With the help of Rash Behari Bose, an Indian nationalist who was for a long term in Japan, the civilian Indian Independence League (IIL) was formed to support the INA and push for Indian independence. This organization provided vital support for the INA throughout the war period. For example, one member in Burma traded liquor for medical supplies desperately needed by the INA. However, tensions developed in late 1942 between Mohan Singh and the Japanese over terms of co-operation. The

---

1 Capt ('General') Mohan Singh had been commissioned in 1/14th Punjab Regt.

Japanese were determined to exercise control over the INA that Mohan Singh was not willing to accept. Thus, he was relieved of his command and imprisoned. Rash Behari Bose was still in good standing with the Japanese, but he had no base of popular following. A more charismatic leader was needed. In May 1943, Subhas Chandra Bose was a leading Congress nationalist from Bengal, who had been working in Germany. He clandestinely left for South-east Asia, on board a German submarine. On the way, he had boarded a Japanese submarine. Bose was instrumental in providing the leadership that was needed at the time. He became

Major Iwaichi Fujiwara (Intelligence Officer) greets Capt ('General') Mohan Singh of Indian National Army (INA) – Singapore, April 1942

Commander of the INA and also set up a provisional government of free India, which was recognized by the Axis powers. The main training camp of the INA was located in Singapore. Young women from the South Asian community in Southeast Asia were recruited for the Women's Regiment, called the 'Rani of Jhansi Regiment'. It was headed by a young medical doctor, Lakshmi Swaminathan, who also became minister for Women's Affairs in the Provisional Government. Bose worked carefully to get soldiers from all communities—Hindus, Muslims, and Sikhs—to cooperate for the greater goal of India's Independence.

Soldiers of INA

In late 1943, Subhas Chandra Bose (given the title of 'Netaji') persuaded the Japanese to attempt an invasion of India from Burma, with the INA as a small force working alongside the Japanese's main invading force. This effort succeeded in breaking into India near Imphal, in 1944. However, the Japanese over-extended their supply lines and lacked air cover. In their opening victories of the war, the Japanese Soldiers of INA had good air cover and succeeded in capturing British supplies as they advanced. But, the battles in the Pacific and elsewhere deprived them of most of their Air Force. The Allied forces in India and Burma were headed by General William Slim. He retreated at first, but then attacked and drove the Japanese and INA from India and back through Burma. Both the Japanese and INA suffered greatly from disease and starvation as they retreated. Some men of INA surrendered, and the remaining troops were eventually captured. The British, Indian, and American forces triumphed in SE Asia, in the spring and summer of 1945.

Soldiers of INA

Netaji Subhas Chandra Bose attempted to escape to Manchuria and was in a Japanese plane that crashed while it was taking off in Taiwan, in August 1945. Evidence shows that during the air-crash, Bose died of burns and was cremated in Taiwan. There was one Indian survivor of the plane crash (Habibur Rahman), and several Japanese survivors. In addition to these survivors, there was a Japanese doctor who treated Bose for severe burns. All the survivors of the air crash and the Japanese doctor were later questioned by an Indian Enquiry Commission, on several occasions. Netaji's ashes were taken to Tokyo and lodged in a Buddhist temple, where they remain even today!

Of the many INA personnel who were captured, three officers of INA, Shah Nawaz Khan (Muslim), Prem Sahgal (Hindu), and G. S. Dhillon (Sikh), were tried for offenses against the British King-Emperor in 1945–1946, in the Red Fort, Delhi. It was a high profile trial and Pt Jawaharlal Nehru represented the INA officers. The trial caught the imagination of the people of India. However, the British had miscalculated grossly, by putting an individual from each religious community on trial. There were massive demonstrations throughout India, and although the three INA officers were convicted and sentenced to transportation for life, they were soon released. The great support of the public for these rebel military officers became one of the major factors in the British Government's decision to grant Independence to India in August 1947.

Bose inspects INA soldiers. Dr Lakshmi Swaminathan is on his right.

'Netaji' takes the salute during an INA parade in Singapore

'Netaji' with his Staff

Postage stamp of INA

www.ingramcontent.com/pod-product-compliance
Lightning Source LLC
Chambersburg PA
CBHW070948180426
43194CB00041B/1794